THE GARDENS

By

Nellie Altamirano-Bustillos

authorHOUSE™

1663 LIBERTY DRIVE, SUITE 200
BLOOMINGTON, INDIANA 47403
(800) 839-8640
WWW.AUTHORHOUSE.COM

First published by AuthorHouse 02/03/05

ISBN: 1-4208-1664-0 (sc)
ISBN: 1-4208-1665-9 (dj)

Library of Congress Control Number: 2004099266

Printed in the United States of America
Bloomington, Indiana

This book is printed on acid-free paper.

DEDICATION

This is dedicated to my Josie, as close in death as in life.

Josie take care of my little angel Dahlia Nellie mi vida.

POR/VIDA

I must thank my friend and mentor, Raquel Rubio-Goldsmith for making me write this book.

My loca friends who put it together, Dr. Ann Marie Hall and Gale Shuesler. I gave them the pages and they somehow put it together.

My children who kept saying "Do it Mom".

And of course Sonny who although thought I was nuts (the jury's still out) left me to my madness.

My always friends Bernice Gasparra, and Terry Lucky. Thanks.

My brothers Arnold and Donald Altamirano who kept me honest.

Love Ya guys!!!

TABLE OF CONTENTS

INTRODUCTION

I hope I might give an inside look into why gangs are formed and the pride and life long bond that made the gang *La Familia*. We have all read of the pattern that can't be broken: poverty breeds poverty. Well that's just not true. I'm here to prove it. Keep an open mind and think how many times you have prejudged people because of race, color, or poverty. Anyone can fall into the hell of poverty and I don't care what kind of background you come from.

I am a Sepulveda, sixth generation Los Angeles Natives, and I am also "Blinky" from Hazard. Who can explain it? The attitude of gang members is *La Familia* because the parents or parent has lost control. The families are dysfunctional with little positive in their lives so the kids start to band together and are out of the house a lot. Gang members like myself share common problems in our lives or homes, and in school where we are looked down. But we want respect. We want to learn to grow up with some values. This is where the gang culture comes in, and turns out to be the only positive thing that is happening in our lives. That is why it is so important to take a gang name, a new name, a new identity. This is a very ancient tribal custom to show you have come of age…that you belong. You have your adult name.

All cultures have done this for thousands of years. The gang values count and are very simple. We have us, we have enemies outside, we have our respect, we have our territory and this is *all* in the world we have. We will protect it, defend it, and form our own culture, our own tribe. The tribe is the only thing that has any value; that's why our family is outside the home. When we go home, what our parents say doesn't mean that much because we have found a new family. We live with our *familia's* values. Many times those values turn out to be self-destructive. Defiance of everything that oppresses you, an immediate kind of defiance, defiance not really made to get us through the long haul. We go into it as children and come out of it, we are told, as adults, sometimes with tragic circumstances. Fighting leads to killing, drugs, and personal annihilation. But in the beginning it serves a valuable need to us. It gives us an identity as a human being, something we can't find anywhere else.

Arnold Altamirano and Nellie Altamirano-Bustillos

C/S

CHAPTER ONE: WHERE WE LIVED

Everyone should have a Josie in her life. A friend who does everything wrong so you look great. Yet she knew so much about life. You know, the "real life". She knew how to live and with great dignity, she died. She was beautiful and yet she made herself ugly. Why? Because she was afraid of the one thing she searched for all her life, LOVE. Boys wanted her and she gave them what they wanted because she thought this was love. Strong dependable men scared her and because of this she always went for the rats. In some ways I guess she took after my mom. She joked about it as we grew older and made a game of it. Her teammates? Bernie and Nellie. Each one in her own game called survival…yep… Jo, Ber, Nel were their names and life was their game.

Josie was the life of the party. The one who got the ride home, drank too much and slept around too much. Well Papa, happy now? Are you proud of your little girls? Josie was my older sister, and this is my story.

I remember Los Angeles as a clean and beautiful city with blue skies and gorgeous mountains. The water at the beaches was blue and the sand clean. When you went on a beach trip, you had no worries. No gangs or crowds. Griffith Park was green without clouds of smog over it. I love Los Angeles and as the song goes "I was Born in East Los Angeles" and what a great place to be. Jews, Japanese, and Mexicans all lived together in one big community. Brooklyn Avenue was filled with fish markets and on Soto Street was their synagogue. Assumption Catholic Church was on Concord and Brooklyn. This was in the 1940's and as the war ended, the Japanese were relocated to a building that looked like a prison on Evergreen and, of course, Brooklyn. What a mix, but that's it folks. All the best loved people in the world in one neighborhood.

At that time East Los Angeles had hills and almost ended at Indiana and Brooklyn. Lorena ran parallel to Indiana and once you passed this you were in a mixture of old and new Los Angeles. First Avenue had many markets that sold fresh chorizo and bakeries that sold warm Mexican bread, *pan dulce*, hand made tortillas, and tamales. We had many parades with horses and *vaqueros* on Indiana and all the floats threw goodies. My Uncle Gil Lopez would always ride the General Mills float and he would throw us little boxes of cereals. During this time a shrine was placed at the Five Points in memory of those Mexican-Americans who died in World War II.

We had family stores on every corner and everyone got credit from the owners. We had a Mexican restaurant with the best burritos I have ever tasted and an old-fashioned ice cream parlor. For twenty-five cents you could get a banana split. The neighborhood was family oriented and children played outside until dark. Families still sat on porches and drank iced tea.

On Brooklyn Avenue houses were on one side of the street and Evergreen Cemetery was on the other. We would play in the cemetery and take short cuts through there, reading headstones as we went. At night the fog sometimes came out of the cemetery and we would scare ourselves silly! The stories we told made the hair on our arms stand up. *La Llorona* was the best and we all saw her coming out of the fog looking for us.

We all have an idea what the perfect way of life is and yet reality brings about a different story. Life for some children is made up of beatings, sexual abuse, and sometimes starvation. You starve not just for food, but love and security. A child is brought into this world and should be nourished with love and a wonderful outlook on life, a life where one could strive for the stars. With some children this is not a reality. You enter this world with a hope and it is driven out of you.

See a look in a child's eye, a smile or that unmistakable look of intelligence and you must grab that child and give him or her a step upward. In 1940 this was unheard of. I don't care who you were, or where you came from, if you were poor no one cared. Society didn't *look* for abuse. We must learn from our past and see where society made its mistake with a whole group of kids that now form the society we call gangs. They have been in existence for as far back as the establishment of neighborhoods. The new gang members take up the cause and get respect the only way they know how, by being the meanest, the mightiest, and letting it be known. *Don't laugh at me, my clothes, my barrio. This could cost you your life.* This is what we learn in our formative years. And who are our teachers? Society.

CHAPTER TWO: WHO WE ARE

The story I write is true and I try to include some good times so you will see how confusing and senseless our lives were. We came from good strong roots, had the advantage of two very intelligent parents, but we were left to survive on our own. Our story is one of many and I wish I could tell them all, but I don't know how many of the girls want their stories told so I will largely concentrate on Josie, Bernie, Terry and me. These are stories I have permission to tell. The four of us formed a friendship that has lasted over fifty years. At first it was a team known as "JoBerNel" that was later joined by Terry Greco.

It is hard to comprehend the full extent of commitment made to your gang or understand the linking of lives to become one in survival. A gang is a family made up of confused and sometimes scared children but kick a dog enough times and it will bite back. In my heart I will always belong to Hazard. A few years ago we had a reunion of the girls; we are still friends and keep in touch as best we can. Of course we are all now grandmothers and have gone through the hell of raising kids. Some of the old Hazard gang have lost children to gang warfare and death and for those, life brought sorrow.

Little Mary's son was shot in the back and is paralyzed. Vicky's son died for crossing the wrong bridge. This does not mean they were gang members but at the wrong place at the wrong time. Vicky is now a great-grandmother and a very successful teacher and administrator. Little Mary is a big wig in Little League in La Puente, California.

Vicky was and will always be one of the closest to me because we go back to Hollenbeck Junior High School in East Los Angeles and I brought her into Hazard. Of course she had to be jumped in[1] and I felt bad for her but she took it. After getting into Hazard she stayed with the group that married the guys from Hazard, while I was with Bernie and Josie. The world was ours. Terry married Pedigo from Flats and so was gone early from our adventures. On with the story…

How can I explain my family? We are so mixed up that I call my family Heinz 57. I think most Mexicans are mixed somewhere in the closet. All I know is we have blonde hair, black hair, blue eyes along with black eyes. White to earth colors.

Dad's side are second-generation citizens (actually first because my Grandma Nellie would not learn English). To my grandma, this was still Mexico. (No, she did not live on welfare.) She remembered history. On my mom's side we are sixth-generation Angelinos. My mom's family came originally from Sinaloa, Mexico. Don Francisco Sepulveda was given land in 1815 by the King of Spain in a vast wilderness. Land which Spain called La Reyna De Los Angeles California. The land went from the mountains on the north to what is now Pico Boulevard on the south. The land reached from the ocean to what is now Westwood Village. This was their Rancho San Vicente y Santa Monica. My great grandfather's ranch was across

---

[1] "Jumped in" refers to a gang initiation rite, which in this case meant the person "jumped in" was beaten up by the gang members.

from Olvera Street where the Los Angeles post-office stands. His land stretched across Union Station.[2]

My great-great grandfather was Jose Dolores Sepulveda married to Louisa Domingo Groningen, the only daughter of John Groningen and Ramunda Feliz (Domingo) Groningen. They had nine children, four daughters and five sons. My great grandmother was their daughter Juana Louisa Sepulveda (known as Louisa). Her sisters were my Aunt Selda, who was born Jriselda Sepulveda, my Aunt Tila, who was born Angelina Sepulveda and Aunt Victoria who was born Victoria Inez Sepulveda. My great grandmother Louisa named one of her children after Victoria Inez, Inez Agnes Sepulveda Reyes.

My great grandmother Louisa married Maurice L. Reyes on July 3, 1886, at the family residence located at 710 Main Street. I understand he was from Reyes Point and was a Deputy Sheriff. His parents were Pablo Reyes and Marie De Los Angeles Lopez. My great grandparents had three children together and their marriage would end in divorce. My great grandfather then married Albertina Reyes. They had a son named Maurice Reyes, Jr.

My great grandmother Louisa gave birth to Inez Agnes Reyes (also known as Aunt Agnes), April 20, 1887; Joseph Reyes (also known as Uncle Joe), June 28, 1888; and William Laurence Reyes (also known as Grandpa William), November 14, 1889. After my grandpa's birth, Louisa filed for divorce. [3] It was final November 23, 1891. My Grandma Louisa was beautiful and strong.

---

[2] I was the keeper of the grant and gave all grants to the University of Arizona Mexican American Research Center mainly because they were falling apart with age but also because I wanted to share the history of Los Angeles. I understand from Antonio Rios Bustamante that he will lend it out to the Gene Autry Museum.

[3] See Case No. 12.111 on December 30, 1989.

My Aunt Agnes moved to Colorado where she died of leukemia. Now my Uncle Joe was a nut and my favorite. This man introduced me to hair in the ears and he was dark like me. He used to tell us how he found his young brother, my grandpa, when he was sixteen. I don't know what happened but Louisa raised my grandpa alone. Do you want to hear the story I heard all my life? I knew you would.

Louisa Sepulveda and Maurice Reyes fell in love but came from fighting families. He, being a Reyes of Reyes Point, California, and she from the Santa Monica Sepulveda's. The boundary line was in dispute and when they fell in love they had to elope. She moved in with the Reyes' and they tried to poison her with lye. She snatched the only baby she had near her (my grandpa William) and ran through the night and when she reached the Sepulveda's, they sent for the doctor. The doctor did the best he could, but she was left with a bad throat and voice. She stayed at the Sepulveda's home that used to stand where the post office is in downtown Los Angeles and across from Olvera Street. That's why my Uncle Joe didn't know he had a brother and when he found out he went looking for him. According to Uncle Joe, he rode the trolley back and forth looking for someone that looked like him. I told you he was funny. No seriously he looked my grandpa up and they remained close all their lives. That is as close as our family can get. We have the worse tempers and can't even play a card game together. My brother Junior (Arnold) would get so mad when we played checkers he would flip the board. My dad hit my mother over the head with the board when he lost. Poor sports. That's us.

My Uncle Joe married Frances Botelo and they had a son Jody. He was paralyzed from the waist down, so Uncle Joe had a car built for him with hand controls. Uncle Joe was the first Fire Chief in Los Angeles and he drove his car just like he was following a fire. My aunt Frances would sit in the back seat of the car and cuss at him as he drove like a mad man on the freeways of Los Angeles; I know he did it on purpose. You know how I know? He did the same to me. He loved to take me to the dentist. Screams of fright all the way; I probably made his day. My Aunt Frances died in her sleep around 1960 and soon after Uncle Joe would stop by my house (after I married) with his lady friends. He would love to tell jokes with double meanings and then he would watch my face for the familiar red. I would ignore him and he would only get worse. This went on until my mom or his lady friend would tell him to stop. "Stop what?" he would say. Oh, he was a wicked man and as I said before, my favorite.

My grandpa used to get jealous and he and Uncle Joe acted like little boys. Each trying to out-do the other. Grandpa use to come over to my house on Ave 29,in the morning for coffee and we would talk. This is when a bond between us was formed. When he held my hairy newborn son after I came home from the hospital in 1964, he said, "You watched too much Beatles, look what you did to him." Grandpa said I was just like my Grandma Josie and he loved my old house. My husband was born in it. Now that's old. I think I was a throw back to the past since I related so well to it. Grandpa lived on Silverlake Drive in Hollywood, I lived in Lincoln Heights. Big difference. My grandpa had a lifetime membership at the brewery on Main Street and I lived near it. Boy, was my husband happy. Grandpa in his sport shorts, high socks, tennis shoes, and be-bop hat. Oh yes, he drove a little Volkswagen. That was my grandpa. When he died I fell apart because I had finally had a close relationship with him and I loved him.

My mom, Margaret Louise Reyes, was born June 30, 1912, to my Grandpa William and his wife Josephine Violet Zepeda Reyes. Mom was a very loved child, along with her brother Edward, and she had a very interesting childhood and her adolescence years must have been exciting. She hung around with the Cano sisters, Flora, Martha and Ruby. She played in their brother's band and everyone thought they would marry. But not mom, that would have made sense. According to my cousin Terry (we were raised like cousins, Flora was her mother), Mom and her Uncle Chuy made beautiful music together. Flora married a fighter named Bobby Herman Greco, Martha married Victor Zamora and Ruby married Louie Montez. What did my mom do? She married a Jewish man by the name of

Johnny Sink. They married in 1931 and for some reason it only lasted a few months. Divorce/annulment - grandpa took care of it. He was pleased to have his baby back. Mama was a spoiled daddy's girl and she liked it like that. She was fifth generation Angelino with a strong family line. Louisa Sepulveda was her grandmother and she had everyone in Los Angeles related to her.

My mother graduated from Roosevelt High School in Los Angeles in 1929 and 30 years later I would follow. She drove a Roadster and played piano, both classical and popular. She was in college and became a legal secretary, all at a time when people were just coming out of the Depression. I have many pictures of Mama and her friends and the Bernals and Felizs.

I never had the chance to meet my grandmother Josie; she died two years before my birth. She was from Tucson, Arizona, and her father, Antonio Zepeda, owned a store on Fifth and Stone. His family was from Santa Maria, Magdelena, Mexico. Her mother was Kathleen Manning Zepeda. After the death of Antonio and Kathleen's two other children, Francisca and Edward, Kathleen gave her child Josephine to Antonio to raise and she returned to Chicago. I never understood, but that is what happened. I have pictures of Antonio and his mother Josefa Montano Zepeda and I guess she helped him raise my Grandma Josie. Grandma Josie was in a convent of the Old Cathedral when the railroad came to Tucson. I don't know how they met or any of the details, but Grandpa said he saw her big black eyes and knew she was his. I do know she and grandpa eloped to San Diego; California when she was 16. They visited Kathleen Manning on their honeymoon. I have a picture of them in Chicago. Grandpa could travel all over the states because he was a Civil Engineer for Southern Pacific Railroad. Grandpa worked half in Tucson and half in Los Angeles until his retirement. My mom would attend schools both in Los Angeles and Tucson. She was in the first graduating class of Roosevelt Elementary in Tucson and also attended Roskruge High School. Grandpa built their house on Ezra Street for Grandma Josie. Her father Antonio would eventually live with them until his death November 3, 1927.

I have no records for my Grandma Nellie (Manuela), but I can tell you what she told me. She was born in Chihuahua and her last name was Rubio. When the *Federales* came, they murdered her father, who was a judge, and her mother. Her older sister, my Aunt Chiyo, took her and joined Pancho Villa. My Aunt Chiyo took care of her little sister and she did the fighting as an *adilita*. My aunt had holes in her face from the rifles back firing. She ran a camp brothel but kept my grandma out of it. My grandma met 36-year-old Juan Lopez, a *solderero*, when she was sixteen and they were married. In order to enter the United States he had to change his name to Altamirano. Because of the War, all people who fought for human rights were considered outlaws by the United States and so many had to change their names. What a shame. We lost a lot of family history because of this. Well anyway, they tried to cross into the states and moved to Juarez, Mexico, where two of their children were born, my Uncle Manuel and my Aunt Romie. They made their way to Nogales and there my Aunt Aurora (my *nina*) was born. They got across the border and had my father, Arnold Altamirano, in Phoenix, Arizona. They made their way to Los Angeles where Juan and Nellie separated. She raised the four children by working at the Central Market in downtown Los Angeles. He went on to Hanford where he mined.

I stayed with my grandma for a while. I don't know why. I will always remember her giving me a bath in a *tina* (thee-na) on the kitchen table. Everyone was there, uncles, cousins, and aunts. Talk about embarrassing. As my grandma washed me she talked and smoked a cigarette and the ashes were just over my head. She never dropped an ash. My grandma always had a cigarette in her mouth and she puffed on it as it dangled on the side of her mouth. While I was on display, I kept wondering how my grandma had teeth in a glass. She kept the glass on the sink in plain view.

My Aunt Chiyo used her money to buy a restaurant called The Carioca on First and Soto. After it would close for the night, the mariachi's would come to my grandma's house and they would party all night. I can still hear my grandma singing Mexican songs.

I would dance around to the music and soon someone would pick me up and dance with me. I was a ham and they loved me for it. My Aunt Aurora took me to see Donald Duck at the show and when I got back to grandma's everyone was there. So what do I do? Of course I walked around quacking and the more they asked me to do it, the more I showed off.

My Aunt Aurora was very nice to me. She recognized the fact that my eye was crossed and took me to a doctor at the General Hospital. I had to wear glasses to try and straighten it. I had my first eye surgery when I was four years old and three more as the years went by. I was left with double vision, and starting school was a nightmare. I still look like a Siamese. My aunt Aurora had red hair and green eyes and wore high feather hats and high heels. My Uncle Gil and Aunt Aurora tried to help us, but it was just hopeless. They could not make much of a difference in our extreme poverty.

I remember Aunt Aurora taking me downtown to buy my confirmation dress; she was my sponsor as well as my *nina*, and she took me to the May Company. They had bras on sale on a table and right there in front of everyone she put one on me over my clothes explaining that you need them so your breasts don't sag. I almost died. I was twelve. I also was taller than her. She is as short as my grandma. That's why the high feathered hats. You know that's how I kept track of her during the ceremony at church. You could see this feather bouncing down the church aisle and I remember it was blue.

My cousin David, was my Aunt Aurora's son. He was from 38th Street and was always in Juvenile. He was slim, handsome, green eyes and black hair. For good measure he had dimples and could whistle the gang whistle by wrapping his lips around his teeth. Whenever he was home from juvenile he would stop to see my mom. He used to draw with colored pencils and he made a picture of my mom that she kept for years. Later, he married Bernice Podovani, our companion, and they had a little girl named Maria Elena. After a few years they divorced and it was a strange situation because I was friends with Bernice and David was my cousin.

My Aunt Romey Tucker stayed away from us but later on in the story you will understand why.

My Uncle Manuel worked for years at the produce market and had two daughters. He died a few years ago of stomach cancer. My aunt took care of Grandpa Juan until he died of stomach cancer and when it was time for his funeral they didn't know how old he was but they knew he was in his late nineties. Grandma told me that is what he gets for taking a young girl. I think she was mad at him. My Uncle Gil has passed and when I saw my Aunt Aurora at Josie's funeral she looked the same. Frisky is how I describe her. My cousin David was there and he had married again. My friend Bernice was amused by the fact that at Josie's funeral she was thrown in with three of her husbands. My cousin David, Mel (a friend of Josie's) and Marty Gasparra, her present husband (and I know last). She found what she wanted after all these years. First, Nana Luisa dies, next came Antonio. Now Grandma Josie gets sick. Her heart value was weak and in those days you died. If it were today she would have lived with a replacement.

During Grandma Josie's illness, my mom meets this charming, uneducated Don Juan. He comforts her and she finds him interesting. He is six feet two, eyes of blue and sandy hair. His name was Arnold Altamirano. He must have known the right words because in 1939 when her mom dies, my mom is pregnant with Josie. My grandpa goes off the deep end and drinks himself into an abyss. My mom turns dependent on my dad and they were married in August 1939. By the time that grandpa knows what is happening it is too late. Poor grandpa, he lost the two women in his life. He tried to make the best of it, giving them the house on Ezra. All my parents had to do was keep up the mortgage payments. My dad couldn't do this and we almost lost the house for nine dollars a month. When things got rough, Dad would drink himself stupid.

CHAPTER THREE: THE STROKE

Josephina Irene Altamirano was born on December 1,1939. She was a beautiful baby. So round and rosy-cheeked. What else would you expect from this perfect couple? I guess we all start out that way. She was born at the Los Angeles General Hospital on State Street. My Grandpa had to admit they did something right. Mom was ten years older than my father and she was the best thing that had happened to this poor, illiterate man. My grandpa intimidated him for good reason while my father used the age difference to his advantage every chance he got. Mom was 29 when she had Josie and eleven months later I followed, and in all modesty, the best thing to come along in 1940. My name is Nellie Margarita. Arnold Jr. was next and he followed eleven months after me. Mom rested for a few years and then had Linda. Eleven months later came the twins, Ronald and Donald. This was the beginning of the end for all of us.

Mom had the twins at St. Marta, a little hospital in East Los Angeles where they believed that if you had to make a choice between baby or mother's life, you had to choose the baby because it had not been baptized. They let my mom labor too long and a blood vessel in the back of the brain hemorrhaged. We all were sent to stay with strangers until Mom could come home. My uncle Eddie and Aunt Dorothy helped care for her. She couldn't move. She just lay there. I remember being home on Ezra Street and then an ambulance came screaming up the street to our house. Mom had another stroke and this time it was bad. A priest was called. Lights, screams, and people. I threw up orange juice and hid behind the sofa and no one even noticed. I remember the smell and I don't know what happened next. Knowing me I probably went to sleep.

Before this time, my few memories of the house on Ezra are warm and I remember the color yellow in the kitchen. Josie and I had our own room and we had a blue bed and dresser with a mirror that went all around the dresser top. We had party paper dolls. Mom painted our room because we had colored our walls with crayolas. I remember my mom as healthy and pretty. She was always cooking and Papa was always there. Mom was always pregnant and always looking sad. We were always acting up and so was my dad. He used us to put Mom in a better mood. Mama couldn't stay mad. To me everything was yellow. Birds use to sing and we always listen to the radio. I guess that's where we learned to use our imagination. A good thing to have as the years went by. On Saturday we would never miss "Let's pretend" nor the song we sang, "If you go out in the woods today, you're in for a big surprise." We would dance and sing and mom would get us dressed and out the door we went.

The air was clean and Los Angeles was a beautiful city. Green grass and clouds. Mom showed us how to look at the sky and see shapes in the clouds. Morieta lived next door and she made dresses and mom had her make some for Josie and me. I remember Mom always granted that life was good and would always be so. Grandpa stopped by every so often to make sure we were okay. Mom would say sure. She was proud then, but should have admitted she made a mistake. According to my cousin Terry, her mom Flora said my mom was happy. Flora, Martha, and Ruby said they hated my dad because he was a womanizer. He flirted openly and drank all the time. It was past socializing. They started to stay away. Mom lost all her friends because they couldn't stand my dad and mom, being the martyr, stood by her man. He was a pro. I think Mom thought that no man could be as bad as they said and they were just jealous and she had the perfect man.

I remember one night while we were listening to the radio. A new song came on and we started dancing to it. It was "Rum and Coca Cola." A conga. We formed a train and danced from room to room. Mama and Papa sat on the sofa with smiles on their faces. Soon the day came to an end and we sat in front of the radio listening to "Inner Sanctum." Off to bed we went and we knew Mama and Papa were smooching. Of course we didn't leave them alone. Josie and I would lay there in bed thinking of ways to interrupt. I remember how warm and safe it felt. The light shining in from the hallway made long lines across the room. I wish life had stayed that way but it had to change. Drastically. I feel that that was the last time I ever felt safe. I grew up fast and with a survivor's instinct that all gang members have. This is what saved Josie, Junior, and me. Josie had her books and Junior and I had each other.

Before mom's stroke after the birth of the twins, she had our little sister Linda. Josie, Junior, and I were playing in the front yard when a cab drives up. It has a picture of a cat on the door. It looks suspicious to me. We stop playing to see what will emerge. The man gets out of the driver's seat and walks around the cab to open the door. Door opens. Mama! We yell as we rush her. She is paying the man and she looks tired. Boy, she is round now. I found out why. It's because God put a baby in her and we are going to have a baby in a few weeks. Mama lets us listen to it. We can feel it knocking to get out. Mama gives us some warm nuts and Josie takes charge of them. She always takes charge. "One for you and one for you and two for me, cause I'm bigger." She dictates. Josie had gotten spanked earlier because Mama told us to plant the carnations and Miss Know-it-all had planted them upside down. Stems stuck up in the air drenched in water. It was a muddy mess. Just as Josie was acting grown up, watering the flowers and all, a boy pops his head over the back fence. He had a cowboy hat and a bandana covering his face. "Who are you?" We ask. "I'm a bandit," he said. That's all we needed. "Mama, Mama, it's a bandit." She comes out into the backyard and just stares at us. "Look, look, there he is!" But no one is there. I think we're in trouble She leans against the doorframe, her big body sighs. We didn't make a sound. No words were needed. Well, we wanted a nap anyway.

Confusion! Mama's gone. Here comes a cab with Papa. The baby's here. It's a girl. Darn, we wanted a boy. Can't we take it back? Mama's home. She sits on the front porch rocking the crying baby. We rush the porch and mama's changing its diaper. We are fascinated by its belly button. Its brown and looks like a string. Mine's not like that, I think smugly. "Oh what a beautiful morning" is being sung on the radio. Mama is wiping this strange belly button of Linda's. All of a sudden it falls off. Oh my God, she broke. We three become sick, scared, and hysterical. Mama made us look at the thing on Linda's tummy. Why it looks like mine now. She holds up the string and explains, a little late, what it is. Well, I guess we can keep her now that she is norm. Back to play. The vegetable man is coming up the street. He has a truck that is open on both sides. Mama takes the baby in and comes out with her purse. She stops him and we yell, "Stop!" just to make sure he heard. He is old and has black and white eyebrows. He gives us peaches wrapped in purple paper. There is a smell of fruit and vegetables that stores of today lack. Yep! I guess I'm getting old. I sound like Mama, always talking about the good old days. Well, back to the stroke . . . eleven months later.

After the ambulance left with my mom, I got my first lesson about people. Them that has keeps and them that don't give. We – Josie, Junior, Linda and I - stayed with Lola who lived across the street from us on Ezra. Catholic Social Services took the twins though we never knew that until they were returned much later. Anyhow, Lola had a million kids yet she had room for us. I thank you Lola and God bless. Lola's house was old and had the home smell. Gas stove and tortillas being made and soup were simmering. She fed everyone and if it moved it ate. Her front yard didn't look like ours; it had dirt. Her house was gray and had stairs leading up to the front porch, which were two stories high. A basement was the first floor. A couch was on the porch and chicken wire kept us safe from falling. A single bulb lit up the front room and shadows danced on the walls. Saints everywhere. Past the front room we found where the smell was coming from. Lola was a big woman and always had a baby in her large arms. Dark complexion, long hair, and dark eyes that looked tired. She worked so hard in her house and no one noticed her. Worn out is what I call it. When we went to bed it was in a room filled with bodies. Warm blankets and kid smells. Feet everywhere and in the middle of the night I got an earache. I was crying softly but no one came. I cried a little louder and still no one noticed. Now I screamed and Lola came into the room with the dim kitchen light behind her and gathered me in her big arms. I remember she was wearing a flannel robe. I was lost in it as she cuddled me. She put olive oil and cotton in my ear and soon the pain was gone. I still use this remedy on my grandchildren. I went to sleep and darn if she didn't put me back in the sea of bodies. Lola's house had dirt and slopes in the back yard and we sent many a chicken flying while I was there. She had a shack that was filled with every child's dream. Old clothes, hats, and old wedding clothes. We played house, wedding, and sang "Lavender Blue."

Josie liked to play these games. What the heck, so did I. We played stage, too. Here is one of the jokes my brother told. He would run in and we would yell "The king's messenger is coming." Of course I was the king.

"King, King, the vipers are coming. The vipers are coming."

"What! The vipers are coming?" I would shout. "Oh, what can we do?"

Junior yells, "I don't know, but he's coming to vipe the vindows." Bad huh? Now I know that some of Lola's kids were zoot suitors, but they would watch us from the porch and laugh. Here they were smoking and bad boys and they liked us. Yes, life was good. In truth I think they thought we were nuts. They brought their girlfriends to watch and boy did they have big hair. Red lipstick and eyebrows painted high and they all chewed gum. Cars were *caruchas*. See? I learned something. In a blink of an eye Mom went from a housewife to a dependant lady and she had six kids to worry about. Oh yes, and the drunk.

Mom was gone a long time and when she came home, it was to a little brown house at 3253 Brooklyn Avenue. Two bedrooms, all the rooms painted pea green. I pass that house sometimes when I'm in Los Angeles and the feelings return. Mom had a brace that went up her left leg and all she could do was sit without help. Mom was told that she would never walk again but she proved them wrong. Our house on Brooklyn was filled with horror but also with love. I think we made the house smile. We continued the stage games and had many adventures with our imagination.

The ambulance would now come three times a week and take mom for physical therapy. Her hand was never used again. This was a shame because of her love of music. She used to play classical piano. She knew them all. We had the only piano in the Barrio. She passed the love of music on to us. She changed the music and rewrote the music so that a one-handed person could play. An example is "Lebensraum." She played it all the time along with "Moonlight Sonata." She tried to teach us all how to play but like most kids we wanted to play outside. All except Josie and Donald. Josie couldn't hack it but Donald played in concert at U.C.L.A. and mom was proud. My father played the guitar and sang Mexican songs. He got the eye of many a woman this way. He was 6"2', blue eyes and could sing like a bird. I was raised with music. All kinds. Now entering my life was Patti Page. What was this new music? I didn't know but I liked it. But I'm rushing ahead. This is easy to do because I have so much to tell.

My father felt so sorry for himself you would have thought it was him paralyzed and confined to bed. Catholic Social Services returned the twins to us and that was the first time we knew where they had been. We nicknamed them Bud (Ronald) and Fud (Donald). Josie got Bud and I got Fud. Mom would wash us from her bed with just a bowl and wash cloth and she would try to comb our hair. She couldn't so we always looked like ragamuffins. Josie and I soon learned, at the ripe old age of six and seven, to wash diapers and hang them out on the clothesline. We would hurry home at noon to feed and change the babies and start to soak the diapers. After we washed them we would play a game. As Josie stood on a chair I would hand her a diaper and a pin and wiggle my butt saying "cigar? Cigarettes?" After we had hung the diapers we would push the line up with a pole. It was bad and it was good.

I remember the lady that lived in back of us. She was as bad as a hornet's nest. She was the sister of the owner and he lived next door. He owned Bell's Cafe, which was one house away. It was never closed. After two, use the back door. This was heaven for my dad. He lived there while we paid the price. There was a path that went from our house to the owner's house around back to the bar. The owner's house was always dark and my mother told me not to go near his house because his wife was sick. Julia was the owner's wife and she was paralyzed worse them my mom. She had white stuff drooling down her chin from her mouth. We were all afraid of her. She just looked creepy. Her husband had a girl friend and would have her as his co-worker at the bar. She had flaming red hair. Then one day Josie and I were passing Jovita's front door and we peeked in. Jovita was there in her wheelchair and she pushed forward making a noise. We looked at her and she motioned for us to come in. We went even though we were scared to death.

This strange woman intrigued us. We opened the door and went in. Josie stayed by the door with her feet ready to run. I remember thinking how awful not to be able to talk. I loved talking. She was thin and bird-like, deep eyes and lashes that were so dark they looked like eye shadow. She wore purple slippers and she had a long petticoat with a black dress and a black lace shawl around her thin shoulders. Her hair was braided and she looked like she wanted to tell us something. All she could do was motion and grunt. Following her finger we looked at this picture of the most beautiful ballerina. It was her! I wiped the white stuff from her mouth and she smiled. She had been a dancer and well off too. She was from Mexico and her family was still there. The property was hers and her husband, Chano, had it all in his control because of her accident. Well that started many visits with her and I learned to care for her. When her husband found out, instead of being mad he gave me sodas to take home. He was glad we kept her out of his way. I would push her outside to see her flowers, red and yellow roses that smelled sweet. Our friendship ended with her death. Boy did things change then. Chano and his sister Dina, began the takeover. They were awful and just because Junior and I sat at the opening at the side of the wood house and lit cotton balls with wooden matches singing at the top of our lungs, "cotton's burning, cotton's burning, fire, fire, fire, fire". Then we would throw the flaming cotton balls under the house. Boy they were mad and boy did we get it. And so was life on Brooklyn Avenue in the 1940's.

Everyone felt sorry for us but it was wasted because being part of a gang of six, we didn't realize we were that poor. I should have known something was wrong when my folks sent all six of us out the night before Halloween trick or treating. Confused people would give us treats. My parents would then give out our treats on Halloween. Or how we would be shoved up a neighbor's fruit tree in the middle of the night to pick fruit. Yep! Something should have told us. We really found out after we started school at Malabar. I think I was in about the second grade when I noticed I was poor. That's when I found out my dad was the neighborhood drunk. Mom was always wearing rose-colored glasses and would tell us lies that she wanted to believe. This is where my Josie got it from. Pretend it's so and it shall be. Josie was the girl in *A Tree Grows in Brooklyn*. She never saw how bad it was. Dad, or "Papa", as he was known when no women were around, would come home drunk and fight with mom so bad and shout so we would all wake up and cry. He loved it. He would hit us or tell us he was going to kill mommy or himself or maybe all of us. Then when he had us all crying he would say he was kidding. The man was sick. One time he came home drunk and after the fighting was over he went into the bedroom and next thing we hear is a gunshot. "No, no" we cry. My mom faints and we keep screaming. He opens the door with a smirk and said it was an accident. He gathered mom in his arms and carried her into their room and we think how romantic. Then my mom screams. He hit her. She came out of the room and he went to sleep. And we wonder why we are a little crazy?

I don't know where I would be if I didn't have my brother Junior. We would escape by going on imaginary trips and as we hiked the hills by Malabar School, we pretend. Blue sky, clean air, and warm winds. That was the life and then we had to go home. We never knew what to expect. Did we have food? Was he drunk? Did we have lights?

CHAPTER FOUR: RELOCATION

I had a frog named Froggie after a radio program and no one could touch him but me. When he died we gave him a funeral with flowers and music. Josie said he was dead. We buried him and all the kids came over. We had a procession and a few girls even cried out loud. Mom got home and screamed "He's not dead he's hibernating!" "Oh! Oh! Now he's dead." We had many friends but we kept them at arm's length because of my father's drinking. Like little adults we knew when to be secretive. We made sure every one leave about the time my Dad should come home. He would swagger and sway and if he wanted more he would go to the bar next door. Women would pay for his drinks. He came home with the smell of perfume and would expect our attention.

About this time the war ended and I remember fire trucks and sirens going off. The Japanese were relocated to an old abandoned school on Wabash. We had many at our school, Malabar, and they tried to mix with us. All the ones we got were from Utah. This was after all the propaganda that was fed to us. These were people who were born here and were Americans, and because of their color and shape of their eyes, were sent away to concentration camps. They lost everything and were ripped out of their homes. Sort of sound familiar? During the depression Americans had to blame someone so Mexican-Americans were sent to Mexico even though they were born in the United States. Men left for work in the morning never to return. They sent them to Mexico in boxcars like animals.

One good thing came of this relocation; I met my friend, Hiroko Nagagawa. She was so shy and she had to care for her two little sisters while her parents worked to get back what was taken from them. I learned to walk in their slippers, and I mean that literally, and to eat with their chopsticks. Her parents were prejudiced against all Americans, though. They had been so hurt. They owned a store on First Street before the war and when they were forced to go to the camps they lost everything. People bought things for nothing because they knew this Japanese family had to sell. A radio for a nickel? Give me a break.

After a while they accepted me. I think it was because I was Mexican and not white - or maybe because they knew we also had it tough in society. We were made to feel ashamed to be Mexican and so most people said they were Spanish or brought out any other lie they could. Most of the old families were guilty of this. At the top of the list was my grandpa. Poor man was in such denial that he missed a lot of life trying to hide who he was. It was acceptable at that time not to speak to your children in Spanish and just speak English in your home. After all you were in America and an American. Most second-generation kids were denied their language and grew up not speaking Spanish. Though Spanish has now been reintroduced into my family through my grandchildren, I feel like my generation was robbed of a right. All the girls in the Gardens at that time spoke little Spanish and if we did it was what I call Zoot Suit Spanish.

As a people, in our infancy we were told we were stupid and made into slaves in our playpen. The Spaniards came and took our land and told us they could handle it better. Next we were told we were ugly because we were not white but the color of the earth. This confused a lot of people who tried to stay out of the sun to avoid tanning. When we tried to walk they said to stoop so we could pick fruit. Now we are learning to run and look out world. For a young race, only five hundred years old, we are learning our right and we are taking back our place in society. Many people don't realize that our race is so young. We began when Cortez mated with Malinche. She is the mother of our race. Their child was the first Mexican. Half Indian and half Spanish. Yes, some of my best friends are Anglo. I was so confused as I grew up because my mom always said we were Irish, Dutch, French, German, and Spanish. Never Mexican. I loved my mom but she had to face the fact that five of her children were involved in the movement in East Los Angeles. Everything exploded and two were so involved that it endangered their lives. We would explain her refusal to face the truth about the way the world looked at us and the lack of education or representation and she finally joined La Raza Unida at the ripe old age of sixty-one and went to Coachella with food and clothing during the strike. Junior was a close friend of Rosalio Munoz and their liberation office was across the street from my mom on Workman in Lincoln Heights. It was in his dad's church and Junior was very active; he is the one that turned me into a militant and activist. That's a whole different story I will get to later. My heroes were the Brown Berets because it was the youth taking a stand. I think we needed them at that time in history. I think we have all become apathetic and we need to look around and see we still have work to do. My opinion.

CHAPTER FIVE: HALF A WOMAN

Mom had to go to the hospital a lot and we never knew when she would be home. It was bad for her but at least she got away from us. The beatings got worse and we learned to hide. Junior and I would hide in the backyard. My father soon learned to leave the house in the morning just like he was going to work. After the ambulance picked up my mom, he would sneak back home with his bottle. Junior and I would sneak under the back window and listen to my father talking to Josie. He was explaining how he was married to half a woman and he needed affection and this Josie could offer him so he didn't go out on my mom. So to keep him home, she would do something. We didn't know what. We didn't understand what was happening. He was raping poor Josie, who loved her "Poppy" so much, almost daily. We told mom about this strange ritual and she got mad at us not him. I never knew what he told her but Junior and I were spanked for lying. We never talked about it again until we were adults, and then it was too late for Josie. Her life was over and would never be normal. It was a disaster. God always watched over me and kept me skinny and dark. Definitely not Poppy's type. I remember one time he was drunk and mom left for her hospital appointment. He was sitting in his chair, now I know, fondling, himself. I had on the only good dress I had and loved. It was red velvet. He said I looked like a gypsy and sent the other kids to school. He told me to change and I stood there looking at him. He looked so different. He tore my dress down the front and I ran outside because I was mad. He tore my best dress. I hid on the side next to the gas station until Mom came home. Yes, God watched over me.

This was the hardest thing to write…it still hurts.

CHAPTER SIX: FAMILY MATTERS

Because mom was not getting any better, Catholic Social Services sent out a housekeeper and boy was she ugly. Dora was her name. She thought she could make us eat raw eggs. She said they were soft boiled but I said raw. After winning that battle, I put the sign in the window for the iceman. It is about 20 by 25 inches with a big "A" in the middle of it. I didn't know what that stood for. I wish mama would get well. We had an icebox and when the ice had melted, we emptied the pan of water under the box. The icebox had a door on the right side for a block of ice and the left side is for food and on top of the right door is a small compartment for butter. Here comes the iceman. He has a big black horse pulling a heavy wagon. The big wheels make a noise on the street. He stops at every house and gets big blocks of ice with huge clamps. He has a cloth over his shoulder. He grabs the clamps and swings the ice onto the cloth. We wait for him to get to our house. Here he is. We run down to the wagon and he chips off some ice for us to chew. On the floor of the wagon lie many ice chips and while he is in the house we collect these. The floor of the wagon is cold and wet. Kids come around and it turns into what we called a snow fight. He comes back and gets in his wagon and with a "shoo" he is gone. That was fun.

Back to the house and it's time to eat lunch. The radio is on and Stella Dallas is having a catastrophe. Mama likes these programs but we know in a little while the happy gang of Buster Brown will be on the air and then Gangbusters. Mama is confined to bed but she still rules the house and knows everything. The housekeeper, ugly Dora, brings us our lunch. Minced ham and cheese sandwiches and Kool-aid. The church sends over the food and boy do we thank them. Dora shuffles around the house with curlers on her head. The meat and cheese are fresh. You know how I know? Because we used to go down to the corner store and have it sliced off the roll for us. I had forgotten the store where so many warm memories come from. It was called Joe's. Joe was a nice older man and his hair was white but his eyebrows were black. He was dark and hair stuck out of his ears and nose. He used to pull his eyebrows together when he was mad. This was a look I got sometimes. He had fruit in boxes outside the doors to the store. It was dark inside and he had a big fan hanging from the roof. Flypaper hung down from the fan and it was always full. In the window he had a sign for shoe polish with a black panther on it. Phillip Morris stood guard at the door. Food and cans covered every inch of his store. My favorite counter was, of course, the candy section. Kits candy one cent. A long piece of paper with stuck on candy, one cent. Now why couldn't mama love Joe? He was nice and he liked us even when we were bad.

My brother Junior and I would sit at Joe's store or take a walk when we knew my dad would be coming home drunk. I would go to the Assumption Church and pray. For some reason I connected the two. You know what really bothers me is why, oh why, didn't someone from the school recognize abuse. If just one person had taken steps we would have been spared so much pain. I think in East Los Angeles at that time it was considered a family matter. What a set up for my dad.

CHAPTER SEVEN: JOSIE

Back to Josie… As time went by, Josie took more and more adult responsibilities and duties. She ran the ship and we were her crew. It's funny and sad at the same time. We were our own keepers and God help the person who picked on one of us. We were the six musketeers and after the life we led, what should we fear? Mere mortals?

One day Josie was on her way home from school and one of Mondo's family hit her and they all said they were going to get us when we passed their house again. Well, this could be a problem because they lived on the corner of Ezra and Brooklyn and we were in a competition over whose family was poorer. I think they led the same kind of life and kept it behind closed doors. We knew. Everyone with that kind of family knows. Well, Mom armed us all with clothes hangers and sent her troop to do battle. We scared them and boy did we get respect. Later, Mondo and I dated for a while. It was by chance that we ran into each other as adults, or rather, teenagers.

Josie was into books and had read *Gone With The Wind* by the time she was ten. She would read her books while sucking on her thumb or drinking syrup. She would sneak brown sugar too. As you can see, she took food as a shield and soon she was fat. But, not too fat for my dad. I wish I had known that this is what was saving her sanity. In those days it was safe for kids to play away from home. Everyone knew you and watched all the kids play. Josie would sit in her room or rather her space and read every romantic book she could get her hands on. She would be transformed into the leading character. She always got this silly look on her face. She was in love with Tony Martin and when he sang she knew it was to her. Scarlet? One of many people she would become. "Josie, come out and play". "No, I must get my rest." Sure. The only time she got out was when we were making scooters out of wood boxes and old roller skates. We would decorate them with bottle tops. You nailed the soda pop tops on and tied ribbons. We were riding them down the hill on Bernal Street and she sashays over because she had a crush on this guy and he was with us. "Oh let me ride on your scooter, please," she cooed, moving her eyes downward ever so slightly. Junior and I just looked at each other. We knew it was Scarlet again. Well, she got her ride and got bit by a Chow where upon her hero rushes her home making noise like a siren and mom poured peroxide on the wound. She would never ride again nor go near a Chow again. Our fun was not to her liking.

Josie was so gullible and would believe anything my dad told her. I remember one time in particular because it was so sick. My mom had to have more surgery and would be gone a few days. She showed Josie and I where she hid twenty dollars in case we had an emergency. That night my dad went out to the bar next door and Josie and I sat by the front door and watched for him. I remember the fog and how it came through the broken window in the door. Josie and I talked about life and what we would do when we met and married a rich prince and would live happily ever after. Then we saw him – with a woman. We ran to our bed, which was the davenport in the front room. He comes in and tells Josie that this woman and her brother had no place to sleep and that he, out of the goodness of his heart, offered them mom's bed. Well golly, that was nice of him. He said they were bashful so we were to look at the wall when they came in. Josie (being Josie) did as he said. Me (being me) peeked. It was a woman! Hmm, there was no man. I knew it.

They get in my mother's room and they start to make noise. Josie and I decided we had to go to the bathroom, which was through the bedroom of noise, and so we knocked. Silence. Finally he says, "Come in" and in his most commanding voice says, "don't turn on the lights because they were still embarrassed." Sure they were. More like bare-ass.

Well in we go and as I hit the light switch in the bathroom he yells. "God damn it, turn it off!" Too late, I saw a pair of blue strap high heels and no men's shoes. When we come out we make a lot of noise and no lights. Into bed we go and who could sleep? Josie drops off. I heard the woman when she left. What a pig! Afterward, he looked down at us to see if we were asleep and I kept my eyes closed. I think he knew I was awake. The next day a man comes to our house with the woman and he yells at my dad in front of the house, something about money. What else is new? I guess he was her pimp. My dad comes in the house and tells Josie and me that this man and his sister still needed money and for just $20 they would sell us their television set. Wasn't this great? Boy, mom would sure be happy. Josie is overjoyed. She wants a television and mom wouldn't mind if she gave him the $20. Wasn't this an emergency? "No! No! Josie!" But she wasn't listening to me. She gets the money and gives it to him. I asked the man, when would we get the set? He looked at me like I was nuts. You know Josie waited by the front door all day for that set. I felt sick for mom.

When mom got home the next day and "dumb dumb" told her what she had done, mom just cried. But good ol' pop...he told her the guy stole the money. He thought he was on the level. Lord have mercy.

As Junior and I ran to school Josie would walk up the hill on the sidewalk. Boring. Junior and I would run and climb and sneak past the old man's house. Everyone knew he's waiting to catch you and when he did, when he did, he would do something so awful. . . he would. Of course no one ever saw him and no one ever got caught. Except for Mary Uribe because she was so frightened that she climbed the fence, which had points on the top, because we thought he was coming. Junior made it, Hiroko made it, Olivia made it, so did I, and there was Mary hanging by her eyebrow. It had pierced the skin. Right through her eyebrow. Yuck. The old man came out to help her and we all screamed. Mary's shaking but is hooked to the fence. All hell breaks loose. He got her down. Her sister came to get her. Mary carried that scar into adulthood. She moved next to me by chance in La Puente when we were old married couples in our thirties. I'll get to that later. Boy did we all get it. You know I was always in trouble.

I would get to school with my hair bow falling off and in those days you had to wear dresses, so of course my "chonies" were always dusty. Josie would walk into Malabar like "here I am". Her bow in place. She had a Dutch boy hair cut with bangs. I had wild hair and mom always tried to put a bow on it, but between my short cuts and fine hair, it would just fall off.

We tried to look like the other kids but we were poor. I didn't feel it as bad as Josie but then no one dared make fun of me. I was little but I was spunky. We could lie and say our father was in the war. What that meant I didn't know. Going home from school was always sad and put off as long as possible. We didn't know what to expect. Did pop go to work or was he drinking? Would we have food or tears? Josie would lead us home and it sounds strange, but we knew by the smell how it was going to be. The house would be dark and still and we knew we were in for it. But if the radio were on, it would be all right. A smell that gives you the chills would pass through us and I didn't want to go in. It got so bad that I would throw-up and go to sleep so I didn't have to see or hear the waiting. It lies heavily on a child's shoulders. Mom would try to feed us with nothing and soon he would appear. He would be drunk and start yelling. "Here I am with half a woman and six kids. What did I do to deserve this?" What did we do? Poor mom. Now I started growing up and I soon became her brace. She had come from such a prestigious family and here she was.

My cousin Terry expressed it well. She said her mom, Flora, would be so sad and mad when she saw what that man had done to my mom. That's how everyone felt except mom. She was happy. She kept her rose-colored glasses on. He could do no wrong. I don't understand to this day. Nobody does. She would put up with anything this man did and excuse him. I think it is sick but I'm glad someone was happy. When mom was a teenager, she and Flora, Ruby and Martha Cano hung around together, and my mom played in their brother Chuy's band. They had a thing. Well...there went another one she passed over for my dad. That's why Terry, Dolly, Kitty, Billy and Bobby were raised as cousins – as close as family could be.

---

4 Harmonica's was a name for music festivals.

CHAPTER EIGHT: THE WARMTH OF THE ALTAR

Class at school was let out early on Wednesday so all the children could attend catechism classes at the Assumption Catholic School. The nuns would line us up in the schoolyard and each nun took about ten kids each. Down the street we would march and I remember their habits flying in the wind and you didn't act up or you would pay the price. Out of respect you didn't misbehave anyway. I loved the way you were educated in the ways of the church and the responsibility was both the parents' and the churches. Now both blame each other and who suffers? The children. I remember I wanted to be a nun and I remember crying when they spoke of the crucifixion of our Lord. The nuns took a liking to me and I learned they were human, soft and nice. The nuns would make it your responsibility to attend church and we wanted to. One Wednesday I was sick so I didn't go to class and went home. I just lay down for a moment and the next thing I knew it was dark and I had a feeling something was wrong. Sure enough, my dad came in drunk. After that, every time I missed church I had the feeling something would go wrong. I know that's the wrong way to think but I was a kid…I think.

About this time the nuns started talking to me about the future. They talked to my mom and offered free Catholic school and she hit the roof. There was no way I would be a nun. I was fascinated by church. The warmth and mysteries of the altar. When our church caught fire I was worried about the tabernacle. I really believed Christ was there. The church use to have free movies in the courtyard. It would be just getting dark and they would set the benches out and show movies like *Saint Bernadette* staring Jennifer Jones. We all were a part of that church and that's why it was safe from any gang attacks. I feel that the kids of today are missing that feeling of ownership and belonging. If they did feel included they would respect and protect the church. I don't care how bad a gang was, we never disrespected the church. We went to the *harmonica's*[4] and dances at the C.Y.O. on Brooklyn as teenagers and there was no vandalizing or fighting in the church or hall. Now outside was something else.

CHAPTER NINE: HOLIDAYS WITH THE AUNTS

Now just as we are learning to survive what happens to us? Once more mom has to go in for more surgery and this time it takes longer. My relatives start taking us in so she will not worry. Junior goes with my Aunt Romey. Josie, Linda and I go with my Aunt Selda and Aunt Tila. They were so old they didn't know what they were getting into. Actually, neither did we. (They were my grandpa's aunts.) They lived in a duplex with an opening between the sides. This way they had their privacy but could be together. My Aunt Selda's son, cousin Winford, lived in a big house next door so he could watch over them. My Aunt Tila had adopted Bernice Easley when she was a little girl and made a bargain with her that if she didn't marry or leave her until she died, she would leave her everything. She did too. I know Bernie is married and living in Mission Bay in San Diego. She earned it, believe me.

This was about Thanksgiving and they took us to a ranch (I think it was the Bernal's) by the Floral Drive-in, and my Aunt Selda said, "Nellie dear, choose what turkey you want." Dumb. I chose the best turkey in the whole place. It stood tall. They gave it to me wrapped in paper with no head. A child's nightmare. I killed it. I didn't eat turkey again until I was married. They couldn't understand why I was crying. Aunt Tila had no patience and reminded me of the witch on the Dutch cleanser can. I know it wasn't a witch but if you didn't show your face, you were a witch. Aunt Selda was so different. She was passive to a fault. She would talk about Uncle Charlie like he was alive. I didn't know him. It was a comedy with poor Bernice having to drive this group home. She drove us all over. We went to Santa Monica to visit someone. I don't know whom, but they lived in a house on the beach. I didn't know they were Sepulveda, but I knew they had money. Next we visited my Aunt Dewey. She lived on Hicks and Olympic. She had a daughter named Flo. Food, food, food. Nobody ran out of food and it was always warm. When we went to sleep I slept with my Aunt Selda. I remember waking up in the middle of the night and seeing fire reflected on the ceiling. I looked and my Aunt Selda was praying. She had an altar in her room and she was saying her rosary. That's when I noticed how old and nice she was. She came to bed and told me that's what I should be doing…guilt.

Aunt Selda's hands shook all the time and she always had a lace hanky in her hand around her fingers. Both sisters always wore black dresses. I don't remember them wearing anything of color. Aunt Tila always moved fast and very seldom smiled. Boy, did we get her mad. She could cook. I'll give her that. Linda and Josie slept in the back bedroom. It was sort of hard just being a kid. We couldn't go outside without permission. They watched us like hawks. It must have been a trip for them. I think they needed a break from us so Winford and his new wife, I don't remember her name, but she had red hair and freckles, took us for a while. This was a novelty to us. Their house was sunshine and reminded me of our house on Ezra Street. In the morning we were sitting in the kitchen and she was cooking breakfast when down the stairs comes Winford and puts his arms around his wife. We giggle and he starts to kiss her. She made him sit down and we had a nice meal with adults talking to each other. Bernice was leaving for work and told us to be ready when she got back because we were going Christmas shopping. People go Christmas shopping? Wow! My Aunts came for us. Aunt Tila was baking beans in the kitchen with a ham bone. I never had baked beans before and they were good. No cheese, or milk. Not fried but good. They also had a new coat with a matching hat for each of us. No way, this was too much! I had never had one, even shoes and a new dress. Those old softies and you couldn't say thank you. Mine was red with a red hat with cherries on it. Linda's was pink with matching hat and Josie's was blue.

CHAPTER TEN: THE VALUE OF MONEY

Now that no one could recognize us, we head off in Bernie's car. She had a new car with a clean smell and it had velvet seats. All three ladies in the front and we three monkeys in the back. We went to Pasadena and in those days it was elite and high society and I can still see the lights and remember looking up in wonderment at the singing Christmas trees. We were rushed along by Aunt Tila and the next thing I know we're back in the car. According to her, they were exhausted. We just looked at each other and held our candy canes, wrapped of course. When we got home we took our baths and went to bed. What a normal life. On Christmas Eve we opened our gifts and everything was practical. I don't remember decorating the tree, but there it was. When we got our stockings they were filled with quarters wrapped in dollar bills, some candy wrapped in orange. Bernice got a big box, I mean big. She opened the first one and there was money and a smaller box. She opened it and there was more money and a smaller box. When she opened that one there was a fur coat. If she is still alive, I wonder if she remembers us. She screamed and that's when I saw it. A smile on Aunt Tila's face! Whoops, it's gone.

The next day Aunt Selda and Aunt Tila had to go somewhere and they sat us down and told us not to open the door and not to move while they were gone. For good measure Aunt Tila told us that the stuffed bobcat next to the fireplace would come alive and eat us if we moved. We didn't move the whole time they were gone. Remember Linda? When they got back they were shocked that we believed them. Ha, ha. Now we are getting bored. We had everything we wanted and if we wanted something, they bought it for us. When the ice cream man would be coming down the street we would run out with our money from our Christmas stockings but before we could get to him, Aunt Tila or Aunt Selda would be there paying for us. Same thing in the stores. Sooooooo! Money had no value to us. They leave us one day just for a little while and we have nothing to do. Linda sticks crayolas in the bathroom sink and Josie and I rip the money in half. When they come through the door I bet they wished that bobcat had come alive. Well, like I said, the money had no meaning to us. They taped them together again after they spanked us. We were crying and they were grumbling under their breath at us. Then they saw the sink. Ladies should not talk like that. My Aunt Selda was keeping my Aunt Tila calm. Thank God they just sent us to bed.

The next morning my Aunt Selda showed us her "Charlie's" razor strap and she hung it in the bathroom and said she would use it on us if we ever did anything like that again. I behaved like and angel. You have to give them credit. They must have been in their late seventies or early eighties. Aunt Tila died a few years later but Aunt Selda lived into her late nineties. I went to her funeral when I was married and had a child, Suzette. I met all the family there and it was the royalty of Los Angeles. I had only met them once before and that was at the D.A.R. Christmas party. Yes, they were members.

CHAPTER ELEVEN: HOME AGAIN

Well, with tears of joy in their eyes my Aunts sent us back to my mom. They acted like they were sad but I know they were glad. Still, I'll bet their lives were boring after we left. I heard Winford got a divorce a few years later and it just seemed so strange that the only normal people we saw together got divorced. Well, divorce seems to run in my family, except with my mom. Now we are home and the twins come home and my dad says Junior is going to stay with Romey for a little while. This was my mom's pride and joy so she kept asking for him. "Tomorrow", he would say. My mom gets upset and calls my Aunt Romey and what do you know? My dad sold Junior to her and her husband! Welcome home, mom. They had to bring him back and as I'm playing outside a truck pulls up and a man comes around and opens the passenger side and Junior gets out in a coat and hat. He had a haircut and everything. I yell "Junior" and he looks at me like I was a stranger. Everyone comes out and mom is on the porch. She can't get down or walk outside. She calls him and he ignores her. He starts crying and wanting to go. I ask him what's wrong and he tells me he wants to go home. I told him he was home. "No, I am Arnold Tinker and I want to go home." What's wrong with this kid? Is he nuts? Poor baby, he stayed by that gate until he was falling asleep. I mean who would want to go somewhere

where it is safe and without the excitement of fighting, drunkenness or adultery? Now it is really getting bad. The drinking now includes my mom. I guess she got tired of fighting it. Now she would hold his arm and go with him to Bell's Café. Now we had two.

The fighting got worse. Well, here comes the funny part so I can put humor into such a hellish life. You know I have a friend who said I always make jokes out of something serious and I said I had to or I would cry. One day Junior and I are looking for something, I don't remember what, and we find a whole box of balloons in my dad's dresser and out we go to the front yard. Now you must remember we live on Brooklyn, one of the busiest streets, and we pass out the balloons to the twins, and to Linda and Josie. Well, we blow up these condoms and we are playing with them in plain view. My mom can't come out and get them. So she's calling us to bring them in. Her voice comes from a curtain as she hides. We ignore her and just keep playing with them until her voice sounded hysterical and we went in. She took all of them away from us and never explained what was wrong. We really thought they were balloons. Life was never boring with us around. Junior and I did so many naughty things that any other mom would have gone crazy. One time Junior and I fried soda pop because we figured it would turn into candy, what a mess. Or the other time I wanted to surprise my mom when she was at the hospital for her appointment. I decided to wash the floor in the kitchen. I get a bucket of water and a box of Tide. Well I had this bubbly mess and it wouldn't go away. I was trying to get it up from the floor but nothing worked, it just kept getting more bubbles. I watched mom and you couldn't describe the look on her face. Finally, she swept it out the back door. Complaint number one thousand from Dina in back.

As time goes by, mom and dad are at Bell's, or rather when my dad wants to take her. She can't walk over by herself and I think that's the only reason she stayed home. She would sit on the porch smoking and watching for him. Do you think he gave a damn? She would beg for attention. I swore then that no man would ever control me. My mom was better looking then the bar flies but that didn't matter, as soon as she got attention from a man or someone would say how intelligent she was, he would remind her that she was paralyzed and half a woman. Mom got him a few times like when he said how he liked to smell women with furs that had strong perfume sprayed on them. She said that was cheap and a lady never would put perfume on a fur. These were the kind of intelligent conversations we had to listen to. Now we had people over. You know the ones who don't want to pay for drinks at the bar. They drank at our house and the smell of whiskey and smoke was always around. Mom passed out a lot because of the medication and drinking. One time her friend was at the house. I'll call her Lupe. While mom passes out, who is in her car messing around outside our house with my dad? Lupe. This happened quite a few times and we saw. Yep, Josie and I saw all.

We got a car. My dad was in Alcoholics Anonymous (A. A.) for three months and we got a car. He worked as a machinist and made good money when he worked. A man named "Price" got him the job and helped him get in A. A. and it seemed to work. We went on picnics and up to the mountains to Hidden Springs and we even fished. Of course I got my dad's finger on a hook. While everyone was eating Jr and I decide to hike up this mountain. Up we go and then we look down. It is a sharp cliff we are on. "I'm not going down, I'll fall." Well, they had to send the ranger up to get us. We named the car Hipsiba, and all six of us fit in it. Of course Josie sat in the front while the rest of us sat in the back. The twins were in a bassinet on the floor of the car and kept jumping up. Well I got a window seat because I got carsick. They learned after one trip when I decorated the side of the car with vomit and from then on I was given lemon drops and a window seat.

That reminds me of the time my dad was working on the car in front of the house. I was in the driver's seat, and I hit the horn and he jumped up and hit his head, the hood fell down, and the knife he held touched the battery. He got shocked and I took one look at this face and took off. I didn't come back for hours. Well, it was all too good to be true. He starts drinking again. Sold the car…back to nothing.

Mom goes back into the hospital and we are left with him. Joe at the store gives us credit for food and I don't think he charged mom what it cost. He will not give my dad anything. Dad is living next door now. One night we hear someone trying to get in and we all huddle together. Troops attack. Junior spills marbles on the floor so whoever it is will fall. Josie and I get knives and Junior gets a meat cleaver and we wait in the darkness for the prowler to get in. We throw on the light and darn it; it's my dad. Drunk and we could have brained him. Who turned on the light?

During this time, Josie has to take care of us and she devised a method that my own daughter used on my kids and that seems to come naturally to all first born. Josie tied us up. One child per leg of the table and there she kept us until mom got home. She would read while we were tied. That poor kid. She had to be an adult at the age of 9, and she loved her poppy. He took her one time to see his father in Hanford and left her in a show when it was light and told her to wait for him. When it got dark she started to cry and the manager called the cops. That's where he found her. With a silver tongue he got away with it. Josie never went again. Oh yes. My grandpa drank like a fish.

I remember one horrible day when my dad and mom called all six of us into the front room and he had that look. We knew someone was going to get it. He took pleasure in handing out punishment. Just like the time Bud (one of the twins) walked and Fud (the other twin, the youngest) couldn't, what did he do? He beat Fud with the strap until he literally ran. Now he called us all in for the same kind of court. Who was it to be? Josie, Junior and I. We had done the unspeakable and visited my Aunt Dorothy and Uncle Eddie who now lived in the house on Ezra. Grandpa let them take it over and my dad said they took it away from us. They had given Linda a pair of shoes that my cousin Ann Marie had outgrown. My dad used this as an excuse to get his jollies. He beat us like dogs and we screamed and cried. Then he made us walk to my Uncle's house and leave the shoes on the porch. When we came out of our house, the owner of the gas station next door was mad and asked if we had been hit. Here we were bruised, crying and still true family. We said no.

The man was so mad and as we went past his business he was yelling at our house. I know my dad was hiding. I still feel thankful that someone cared. He was Japanese and was not well liked because of the war and yet he stuck his neck out. Says something about people.

The war changed all our lives and made heroes of many of our neighbors. Every home had a flag, which meant they had someone in the war. Not us. My dad hid behind us. See we came in handy for something. This did not prevent him from telling us how he was to be sent off to war and he might die. Lies. He just wanted to see us cry. The man was sick.

The time I write of is when Lorena was the end of Los Angeles and you could see the San Gabriel Mountains. The sky was so clear. Dirt streets were common and stores had flypaper and goats' heads in the meat windows. City Hall was the tallest building and really the only building. We would catch the streetcar to go to town and it was a nickel. Wood chairs and bells. Open windows and sliding doors, half glass, to separate half the streetcar. Not because of color but because it looked good. Mexicans were not blatantly discriminated against but it was there. We would dress up to go downtown. We had many hills in our part of town. Now they are all covered with apartments and stores. We had short cuts that would take us through pipes and over fences and along paths that had fig trees or apricots. You ate better on the street than you did at home - the orange juice factory where we got soft oranges and the bakery with paper cones filled with candy (frosting) and fresh tortillas made at the *tortilleria.* They gave them warm to all the kids.

CHAPTER TWELVE: POORER THAN THE POOREST

We were being kicked out of our house on Brooklyn and my dad said not to worry because he had another job just waiting for him in Honolulu. He went one weekend by himself to get all the details. He tells us that they want us all there and that they have a house for us. Furniture and all. Since it is too expensive to ship our old furniture my mother sold her furniture. She gave the money to my father to hold. She really believed him. Her furniture and nick nacs were all she had linking her to the past. She said goodbye to all her friends and they wished her well. We were all packed and out on our porch waiting for the taxi the company was going to send. My dad couldn't understand why they were late. He would go next door and call them, whoever they were, and come back and tell us there was a delay because the ship had barnacles on the bottom and they were scraping them off. Dumb? Yes, but I think my mother wanted to believe so bad that she kept pretending to believe him. Soon after midnight he tells us the barnacles were too thick on the ship that we couldn't leave right away. Mom cried. She knew.

So, as I said, we had to move. I left my good friends and moved to Union Street. This is on the West Side of Los Angeles. We lived at 1708 Union near Washington Street. We went to Norwood and we were poorer than the poorest. Our lights were turned off and my father taught Josie how to put a penny in the fuse box and we had free lights.

We had no curtains so papa put Bon Ami on the windows and the smell of jasmine was all over. Our house was an old house that should have been condemned. It was next to the sidewalk and had some jasmine plants on both sides of the porch. It was two stories and like all the other houses must have been built back in the 1800s. It had stables in the back but a fence had been built to separate us. It now was used as an empty lot for parking. Next door to us lived a black family by the name of Washington. My friend and schoolmate was Roosevelt Washington. Yep, two president's names. This was our first experience living with blacks and at first a strange one until the color disappears…and it does. Dixie was a white girl who hung out with us. Two houses down lived the Ortiz family with a child to match the ages of our family. Eva was my friend and Neito was her brother and my first crush.

We found out that there was a night life. A center called Toberman Playground was haven for the kids in the neighborhood. We would go on free trips including ice-skating that turned out to be my favorite. There was basketball with all the guys in the neighborhood having games every night. This took us out of the house and away from the nightmare going on there. Between papa's drinking and the dark house, Toberman'st seemed an escape for us. The playground was full at night and when we left the house mom would be sitting on the front porch with her cigarettes and the smell of jasmine was all over. We would play until bedtime and walk home in the dark. It was only a block away and all six of us made a group. Then my father started coming with us. He wanted to be with his kids? No, Miss Jenson was there and felt sorry for him. They visited many a night. We couldn't care less. Josie had bloomed and was now a lady. Yep, she had started her menstruation. Wowie! Let me tell you how it came about.

Mom never talked sex, women's bodies or anything resembling the birds and the bees. So here was Josie at John Adams Junior High and when she went to get up she was bleeding and of course, she thought she had hurt herself. The teacher told her to come with her down to the nurse's office. The nurse had to explain and show her how to use a Kotex. Talk about humiliation. They gave her a skirt and sent her home and when she walked in, I was home sick. She walked right by everyone and went to her room. This was the back porch upstairs. She was mad and all Junior and I could get was something about "administration." Poor Jo.

Well the boys started noticing her and she loved it. She would go for walks with them and she kissed them. I know because Junior and I spied. We had an old deserted house by the playground that was three stories high and everyone went there on a dare one night. We told scary stories and went for a hunt for ghost and we were scared. Everyone was jumping out at people and trying to scare them. I admit I was scared. The house smelled old and was so dark the only light that came in was from the playground so you only saw shadows. The older boys were trying to grab the older girls; thank God I was a babe. Then the fun stopped because all the couples started messing around and we watched Josie. She thought she was so mature. It was still innocent and exciting.

Soon other boys started coming around and Josie was at long last her Scarlet and she knew she was pretty. She really was but I would never tell her that. Now boys started to come over to play with me but I know why. It was to see Josie. Oh well. I still was their best friend.

About this time I found out there was no Santa. because I saw my dad come home drunk and tell his starving family about the thick steak he had had for dinner and then proceed to toss out our Christmas presents into the street. He was yelling about charity and the gifts that were given to us by the Salvation Army. Mom had hid them in the closet downstairs. He took the gift we had for him and opened the box. A tie, a measly tie. He threw that into the street too.

Union Street was a busy street and our gifts were soon smashed. We salvaged some but they went to the twins and Linda because they had been asleep and were too young to be disappointed. Josie didn't care because she got her lipstick and that was all she wanted. It was called Tangee and every girl stated with that lipstick. She was so excited about it you would have thought it was made of gold.

Now I started noticing boys and found I was their best friend. That, I learned, was to be my fate until I bloomed. I remember one in particular by the name of Nieto. He was my friend Eva's brother. When I was sick he left a bottle of "Evening in Paris" on my back door with a little note and then my bubble burst and his sister told me he took it from his mom. But it was the thought that counted, right? I was a very sickly child. Between the surgery on my eyes and my weak stomach I was always under a doctor's care. They gave me vitamins and tonics to gain weight and the tonic was chocolate syrup and it would disappear somewhere and we found it under Josie's bed. I was small for my age and thin and I think the thinness came from nerves.

At Toberman Playground I heard the word *gang* for the first time. They were called Los Gatos and they hung around the playground at night. Smoking and chewing gum. They had white,white shoes and looked like they had it together. The guys had ducktail haircuts with Three Flowers pomade on their hair. They wore khaki pants, leather or blue suede jackets. They chewed fan-tan. They always had a cigarette in their mouths or a wood match. I knew some of them and as we played, they left us alone. Of course, it helped that some were the older brothers and sisters of the kids in our group so if they touched us we would tell their moms. Josie was too young for them and she was actually a square. I remember one dance they had at the playground and my dad took her. Well when he took her out to dance, she tried to lead. Of course he insisted on taking her to all the dances even if she didn't want to go, so he could chitchat with Miss Jensen.

On Christmas we all were in the Christmas play and my family had almost all the parts. Junior, Linda and I were the three kings and sang "We Three Kings" as we walked down the middle aisle of the auditorium. The twins were shepherds and Josie was an angel. The inside joke we all had was that the girl playing Mary was pregnant and none of the adults knew. We had so many activities at Toberman that this is why I believe we stayed out of trouble. I used to walk up and down the streets and no one bothered me. As I said before, kids were safe then or else my guardian angel really watched over me. I crossed busy streets, like Washington, Pico and even Union, and though I was only nine or ten, I never got hit. I use to walk to church, a habit I got into on Brooklyn, which was on Figueroa. Santa Monica Church was huge and one Good Friday I walked there for the mass and when I came out it was cloudy and I remember thinking God was mad at what we had done to his son. It started to rain and I got scared. Loquat trees were in bloom and as I walked I ate some.. You could pick the fruit off the trees and eat them as you walked. I really wanted to be by myself and that habit I hung on to.

As time went by I became more aware of the cruelty of my dad and tried to stay away from him. He would stay away from home for days and then come home with a lame excuse that mom would accept. I started to think all men were like this. I remember one time he was in jail and mom made Josie and I take a note to this woman. She read it and you could see the pity she felt for us. She dropped the charges. It seems he had taken her home from a bar and then when she told him to leave he got violent and she called the cops. That's when Josie and I knew we were the adults in the family. Well, we could go no lower and we knew it. I think that was the worst part…knowing. We now had no food and no rent. Gas? Lights? Water? No way. We used to sneak over to neighbors' homes and as they watched television we would fill our pans with water from their hoses. They never knew. We would then take them home and that was our drinking water. A lot of people did that and so if you hear your water running outside, leave it be.

I started to work for Mrs. Burnett and she would pay me to clean her house and watch her son. I didn't want to go home after a day in that clean warm house. Food was always plentiful because Mr. and Mrs. Burnett owned a hot dog stand. I didn't really clean; it was more like keeping their son entertained. I would get paid five dollars a week and give it to mom. Of course she would give it to my dad. He in turn would give it to the bars on Pico Blvd. It was only five dollars but it was a fortune to us. The Burnett's treated me well and they would take me to the show or out on outings and keep me overnight. On those nights I slept in a big bed all by myself and I remember the clean smell of sheets and I would be in the middle of the bed feeling like a princess. They bought me clothes to wear when we went somewhere but I had to leave them there. I guess they knew my dad, too. I wanted that kind of life and I made up my mind I would get it. Silly,silly me. The best was yet to come.

CHAPTER THIRTEEN: RAMONA GARDENS

A dangerous play was in the making and it was being formed in my father's head. You see Shorty (my dad as I called him now) had come up with a plan that would get him off the hook forever. What he told my mom was that until we got on our feet she should apply for Aid for Dependant Children, known in the inner circle as state aid. Then, once he made our fortune he could take us all to this great house and we would have food and no worries. Sure. Now mom believed him and in those days you could not have your husband, boyfriend, or any man living with you in order to collect. Of course this meant that Shorty would become our Uncle helping mom move and get settled. He told them his name was Bob, and that he was Arnold's brother. Of course this meant that he had to move in with my grandmother so they wouldn't get suspicious. Grandma Nellie was sweet but when it came to her baby boy she was a tigress. She had always thought my mom had taken advantage of her son and so she was overjoyed to have him back. He had a great time there and would tell us all about it.

In those days you were investigated and watched to make sure no males lived with you and after a few weeks, I guess they figured no man would let his family live in such poverty. They took over. They gave us food and told us we were to move to a project. It was on the East Side…and so the best began. First off we were returning to the East Side of Los Angeles and second to a house with lights and gas and water. Oh Heaven be praised. We would return to our families' side of town and family support.

You know people always complain about housing projects? I'll tell you, it looked like paradise to me. The name was Ramona Gardens. We had gotten up early that morning and loaded up a friend of my dad's car. I remember his name was Lennie O'Brian. There was a trailer attached and we put our junk in it. We had been told that the county had gotten us some new furniture and it would be at our new home. A stove and refrigerator came with the house. My dad helped us move because he was now Uncle Bob or "Shorty," his new nickname. We started down Pico and used it to get to Soto. East to Zonal and as I saw Brooklyn Avenue I knew I was home. We passed over the Bridge just past Wabash and Marengo and we turned right on Zonal. At this time there was just an empty lot on the corner and a curved street that led past the Santa Teresita Church and School. At Lancaster we turned right and continued until we turned right to Indiana up to our unit "Ruez Lane".

This couldn't be it. Green grass. Two story units with fences and clean lanes Separating the units. I still remember driving up to this end house with trees and grass and the magic number 1527. Yep, this was it. I knew I was home. We ran to the front door and when we opened it, it smelled like fresh paint. It was white and the state had given us some furniture and it was clean. The kitchen set was wood and the beds were basic wood beds but to me they were beautiful. I had a bed. The kitchen had a gas stove and a refrigerator and they worked. The gas was on and the lights all worked. A pantry for food, oh it was Heaven. Josie and I were so excited that we laughed and Cried and turned on the radio. Yes, it worked! Turned on the water and next we put together our room. We still needed clothes but now we had a dresser to put them in and a closet to hang them in. Our window looked out at a tree and you could see Indiana Street from there. God, it was great. My brothers had their own room, too, and the state gave them bunk beds along with a single so each had his own bed. Here was the best - mom was single. They gave her a bed for her and Linda. At first that's how it worked out because dad said you never knew if "they" were watching. He stayed with grandma. That is until he saw how comfortable we were. Then he came back and we were told to tell everyone he slept on the sofa downstairs. It was because my mom needed help and he was a good uncle.

I think I fell asleep that night with a smile on my face. We had a linen closet in the hall that was filled with linens and we had real sheets and blankets. We could even take a bath before bed. As I said, the best part was my dad had to say away. Yes, life was good again.

CHAPTER FOURTEEN: BERNIE

Fate was at work as I slept and was sweeping me into lifelong friendships that now have lasted over 50 years. As I was living my wonderful life way across the United States, a little girl was trying to grow up in New York. Her name was Bernice Podovani and she was half-Italian and half Puerto Rican. Her earliest memories of course are of sitting on her stoop watching all the guys at the candy store. Who knows? They were probably buying or selling. They were all cute and young and in those days they were a mix of nationalities. This is the one memory that stands out. Bernie and Josie were cut out of the same cloth so this would be something that she would remember. Bernie was soon to join Josie and me as tomboyish, daring and yet the *femme fatale.* This was Bernie.

Bernie remembers the blackout during the war when her mom would put her and her brothers and sister, Richard, Paul and Betty, in a room and she would be frightened but her mother would reassure her that everything would be all right. Bernie's mom, Esperanza, stood a whole 4 feet 10 inches and so Bernie didn't quite have the confidence she needed as she heard the sirens and she didn't understand the noise, only the confusion. She was afraid that the planes would come and drop the bombs. I think this was a shared fear of everyone living near a coast. You had to shut your curtains and everything had to be black. No lights. That's what made it so scary. Ha! Ha. We didn't have to worry. We had no lights.

Her dad was also cut of the same pattern as my dad. Actually all the girls in the "Gardens," as the projects were called, had great dads just like mine. This is the first stitch in the pattern. Next comes the adult role and looking out for yourself and survival.

Bernie remembers that her dad had been gone and they didn't know where he was and they started getting worried. I asked her, "How long was gone? A day or two?"

"No, Nellie…months."

I started laughing. Her mom was one of the sweetest shyest ladies you could meet and did not speak English that well. She was not an aggressive woman. She didn't question him or his absence. Of course, months is sort of pushing it. Anyway, a friend told her to go to the Red Cross and they would help her find him. Well, son of a gun, he was in the service. He never told her, he just went. He had lied and said he was single. The Army gives Mrs. Podovani all the back pay she had coming to her and when she received this big check, she was so excited that she said she would use it to go to California.

This she would do with or without him. That's how they landed in the Gardens. Bernie moved in two units away. Her mom packed them all up when she got her check and the funny thing is, Bernie remembers the train ride across the nation. Her mother with this big bag stuffed with dried fish, crackers, cheese, salami and things that didn't spoil and all the children seated near her. Now we're talking about Bernie. Well she looks over the situation and decides this is not her cup of tea. She spots her victims. A young, childless couple. Uniform, that's good. So, she hooks up with them, of course mentioning her dad is in the same uniform, and she talks her way into meals and comfort on the ride to California. When they would come back from the diner she looked at her family eating from their bag and decided she would stay close to the young couple. From New York to Los Angeles she stuck like glue. She was Bernie.

Yep, a survivor.

Bernie had many family connections in Los Angeles and so she and her family had help in getting on state aid and moving to the Gardens. Talking with Bernie I feel she has blocked out many years as we all do when it's not good to think of our past. Her father was very abusive and eventually joined them. She is not sure, but she thinks before they came to the Gardens they lived in San Francisco. It's a blank in her mind. She does remember her dad hitting Betty, her sister, and hitting her like a man. Bernie's sister was a true *pachuca* and I had heard stories about her being bad. While in San Francisco her dad tried to take over but the older kids were too old not to resent this. Mrs. Podovani had two more children, Lydia and Johnny, and then her dad was gone again. That's when they moved to the Gardens. By then Betty would take off to New York every chance she got. In the Gardens they called her "Boxer" and she hung around with a girl called German. She was on heroin and back in New York on one of her trips she married another hype[5]. They had five or six kids (I've met two and they are just as beautiful as their mother pictures). While trying to get away from the cops, she hid in an old building after jumping from building top to building top, and they found her dead with a hypodermic needle stuck in her armpit. I guess she hid it. See we all were normal.

Bernie and her brother Paul started Murchison Elementary about the same time I did. We didn't cross paths yet but very soon she would become as close as a sister to both Josie and me. Bernie, silly, strange, and yet one of the strongest people I know. Bernie remembers when she saw the projects for the first time and they were all green grass, space and cleanliness. You who have the luxury

---

[5] Hype is a nickname for heroin addict – addicted to hypodermic needles.

of a normal house will never understand our feelings as we first saw the Gardens. Life changed and we knew we had a chance. At what, we were to find out later.

CHAPTER FIFTEEN: IN THE GARDENS YOU RAN LIKE A PACK

As I opened my eyes the sun was shining into my room and as I stretched I was contented. I ran downstairs. Mom was making breakfast like a real family. She needed a few things from the store and she asked our new neighbor where it was. She said follow the street and it will lead you to Venegas store. Well, Josie and I had to go and as we left the house we noticed three black girls looking at us and making sounds at us. We were used to being the new kids on the block so we just waved and went on our way. We found the store and carrying bags, headed for home. Well, there they were. Waiting for us. The three had now become four and a small group of kids had gathered. "Fight, fight" they yelled. First they hit Josie and I dropped the bag and we fought. Damn, we were good. We rolled around and hit and soon everyone was exhausted. We never had to fight them again. In fact, we all became one group. Levy and I became best tomboy friends. Her family was Watuzi and they were all tall and beautiful. Fine features and they carried themselves proud.

In the Gardens you ran like a pack and you played all the normal games that all kids do. Skating was fantastic because of the lanes. You could skate just like roller derby and we had some pretty rough games. Mrs. Gaston would yell at us to shut up and come out of her house with her broom. She must have been at least 250 lbs. and she would always beat her husband with her fist. He was a small drunk. It was a great time for me. We would all go over to the empty lot across Indiana and roast potatoes in the ground with a bonfire. We would pretend to smoke these weed rods and as night fell we all sat around with the factory smells and stars around us. It was a magic time and we were lucky to have lived then. It was still safe. We didn't go home until nine or so and no one missed us. The Good Humor man would come down Indiana and we would get chocolate mint bars. Of course we shared. All the girls wore their brother's clothes and I lived in jeans and T-shirts. I could climb the highest tree and outrun even Eddie Joe Brown. He hated me. I don't know why except I had a big mouth and made fun of him once. He would not accept my apology. Instead he would wait every day for me to be coming home from school and jump out at me. He was big. I would start running with him right behind me snorting and when I would get to my house the stupid door would be locked. I'd pound and jump over the fence to our back yard. Eddie couldn't jump as fast, and our house being the end house had a "T" shaped fence, so I would jump one, jump one, knock and scream, jump one, jump one until mom would open the door. I would stand there with a smile and wave at Eddie and knew he would be waiting the next day. This went on for about a month and then my mom made me apologize in front of everyone. No fun. One thing I always did was go home straight from school. See I was good.

This is how I began 1950. A good year. One full of discoveries and growing up. Yep ten was a grown up. My dad (a.k.a. "Uncle Shorty") was with us most of the time and also with my Grandma Nellie. He would come over with fruit and bread from my Grandma and all the neighbors thought he was the greatest Uncle in the world. There was one in particular that always seemed to be in her doorway when he would come. Her name was Louise. She had three boys. Gus, Skipper, and Tiny. They always played with us and Gus was in my group of friends. One day my dad was walking down the lane with his arms full and I yelled "Papa" and he turned beet red and grabbed my arm and pushed me into the house where he beat the daylights out of me. He said his name was Shorty and someone might have heard and would report us. Mom tried to explain to me how important it was to keep up the pretense. I hated him. I was never to call him dad again.

Of course this was because he had started an affair with Louise our next door neighbor (always at our house). We saw him a few times coming out of her house and we kept it from mom. We knew she couldn't take it. Our friends were all talking about my Uncle Shorty and Gus's mom, and even Gus told us. Still we kept it from her. Then one day he came down the lane with his arms full and turns into her house. Gus and his brothers called his name and ran to him. Josie cried and mom put a glass to the wall to listen if he was next door. She still couldn't comprehend that he could do this to her. Next she goes crazy and makes Josie and I take her next door. She couldn't walk on her own. When we got to the front door, the other neighbors stayed indoors out of embarrassment for us. She pounds on the door. We could see him sitting on the couch with his arm around her. This was too much. Mom opens the door and tells him he must choose. What a joke. Here he sat comfortable and tells us she is pregnant. The love of his life. Mom slaps him and we take her out crying.

I think she was a little off the next year. She would drink, home delivery from Venegas, and yell at the wall. She tortured herself with the glass on the wall and would listen to them, even in bed. She would call us to listen. She lost a lot of weight and this she could not afford to do. She only weighed about 100 lbs. and that was with her brace on. Well, it got so bad that Louise had to move. You couldn't be pregnant and be there without a husband. My dad moved her and her group out and the worst part was, it left it open for him to visit my mom. Louise was not around. Mom, of course, took him in. Mom fell for the line that he just wanted to be a part of the baby's life because it was not the baby's fault what they had done. What does mom do? She buys them a bassinet. Honest. That's okay; we got it back later and put it to good use.

The twins had their friends and Linda had her group. Shirley and Alex lived across the lane from us and they hung out with us when they lived there with their mom and her boyfriend. Her family had the sharpest feature I have ever seen on black people. Beautiful smiles and healthy teeth. You know how they got them so white? Chicken bones and baking soda. Yep, after they ate chicken they walked around with the bone in their mouths and chewed on them. First you dipped them in baking soda. Well we all picked up that habit and I didn't have my first cavity until I was seventeen. The only problem I had was when they would get a chicken and all the gang gathered around, and Alex's step dad would swing it over his head, snapping its neck, and toss it to the ground. We would all scream and watch it run around until it died. When their dad would pick them up for a visit, they would come back all clean and with new clothes. It took them a while to get back into the swing of things. Then here he would come and get them again. In our unit, I think after Louise left we were the only Mexicans. Everyone else was black. We saw no color. We would all walk to Lincoln Park and fish with strings and safety pins. It works. We would catch catfish and use their eyes for bait. Shirley's family would fry them up and eat them. Junior hung around with us then but he was short and wore glasses and soon had the nickname "professor". This stayed with him until high school. He would walk with us to the playground and hop freights with us but always with this attitude that said "if you try to leave me behind I'll tell mom what you are doing." This also stayed with him until high school.

Looking back at the conditions and lack of value which society put on our lives, I'm appalled. We had a playground in the middle of the project adjacent to railroad tracks and no fence to keep the kids off the trains or children from playing on these tracks. We had open sewer streams with pipes crossing over. Of course we had to walk these pipes and one day I fell in and sewage engulfed me. Everyone pulled me out and then I had to walk home with a group of kids telling me "You'll be all right." Sure, it wasn't them smelling like doo doo and dripping it along the way. I know of no other way to say it. When I got home I went to the bathroom and ran a bath, stripped off my clothes and took a boiling bath. Emptied the tub and repeated this over and over. I couldn't scrub hard enough. I must have taken four baths that night. By the next morning everyone had heard about it. I went through all the jokes and comments and I couldn't even fight back because I would have done the same thing if it had been someone else. I think I'll take a bath. Yucky!

CHAPTER SIXTEEN: BOYS' DAY OUT (AS RECALLED BY MY BROTHER JUNIOR)

I was about eleven years old, maybe twelve, and Bud and Fud were about eight years old going on nine. We lived in Ramona Gardens Housing Project in northeastern Los Angeles, half way between East Los Angeles and Lincoln Heights. It was summer vacation, school was out, and we used to go from the housing project in Ramona Gardens over to the Variety Boys' Club in East Los Angeles. To get there we used to walk and cross over this newly constructed bridge that went over the San Bernadino Freeway and down the street about two miles to get to the club. We would go there and, you know, get in trouble, horse around, play pool and then come back later on in the day. One day we were going down there, along Fickett Street - the main street we would go west on to get to the Variety Boys Club - and there was a little mom and pop grocery store on the corner where we would stop and maybe buy a candy bar or something like that. If we had any money. An older couple, this huge, huge imposing, mean, ugly-looking old woman and a guy who was small and meek, ran it. Basically, she ran the store.

Anyway, on our way down Fickett Street to the Club, on the opposite side of the street from the store, there was a bank of about three garages sort of built into the side of a hill. These were directly across the street from the grocery store and as we were walking by I happened to look at the garages and on one of the door hasps that locks the door, there was just a stick stuck in the hasp, no lock. So being curious and up to mischief at that age, like you always are at that time, especially when the streets are your playgrounds and the only fun you have is when you are doing something you're not supposed to be doing, I just very quickly stopped and pulled the stick out and opened the garage door and looked inside. Lo and behold! It was the garage where they stored all the beer, wine and sodas that were sold in the store across the street. I looked in and it was like looking at paradise, nothing but bottles all over the place and, of course being that age, I didn't even look at the beer or the wine bottles. All I saw was a bunch of bottles of s-o-d-a! Pepsi and Dad's Old Fashioned Root Beer. Anyway, I close the door real quick, put the stick back in and then join my brothers and go to the club. While we are there we decide to plan the caper! We were going to be a gang of three and we were going to pull a heist on the garage on our way home. We had it planned out really well. I made the plan and my two brothers would hopefully do what they were supposed to do.

The idea was that Fud would go ahead of us up to the store and stake himself out. There were a couple of small steps that led up into the store and he would look inside and Bud and I would hang around a little further on down the street. Then Fud would give us the "hi" sign when the lady or the man or both of them were preoccupied in the store. When he gave us the "hi" sign, we were going to scoot into the garage and load up with all the sodas we could carry and take them home with us. Then when we were loaded up and ready to go, I was going to look out of the crack in the door and give my brother a sign to let him know that we were ready to come out. He would give us the safe sign when nobody was looking. Then off we would go and hey we would have all the soda we could drink. Anyway, that was the plan.

We were coming home and Fud went ahead of us and sat on the stairs looking into the store. He gave us the "hi" sign. So Bud and I go real quick up to the garage door, take the stick out, and close the door behind us. We totally ignored everything except the sodas that were there, which was fine. We loaded ourselves up, but we didn't bring anything to carry them in so we were basically loading up our arms, stuffing our pockets and the inside of our pants with as many sodas as we could carry. Soda's back then were in bottles. We were so loaded up that we could barely just waddle. I went "clanking" to the garage door to take a look outside to open it and make sure nobody would see us, and then check on what my brother was doing so he could give us the "hi" sign to come out. I open the door and my brother Fud is sitting on the steps looking down the street in the opposite direction of the garage, daydreaming about something, who knows what, but he has just totally blown his assignment. At the same time, coming across the street toward us looking bigger than a bull elephant was this unbelievably huge woman. I don't know if she was Russian or Jewish or something like that…European woman… storming across the street as fast as she could go TOWARD US! I had no idea what to do. Here we were trapped in the garage, and here she was coming across the street and without thinking I just absolutely panicked.

Now, Bud was behind me and I just yelled "Bud, run!" I threw open the garage doors as hard as I could, which stopped her in her tracks, and the two of us come charging out and start heading down the street north as fast as we could go, which was not very fast because we were loaded down with all these bottles! We were trying to hold them in our pockets and in our arms and keep them stuffed in our pants and we're running down the street like a couple of ducks that have to go to the bathroom real bad and this lady, because of the way we're running, she's really not much slower than we are, so she's chasing us, and meanwhile Fud has disappeared somewhere. God only knows where he is. My brother Bud and I are running the best we can and we're not really getting away from her and she's right behind us so we run around the corner, make a right and we're waddling down that street and she is still after us yelling "stop. Thieves" and all this kind of stuff and we had gone down the street about three or four houses and sure enough, there are about half a dozen guys (13 or 15 year olds) sitting on a porch. They look at us going by and they see her coming behind us. Meanwhile, we're losing bottles left and right and they're hitting the ground like hand grenades going off, broken glass and soda all over the damn sidewalk, but we're getting lighter and beginning to move faster, so these guys, just for the hell of it, decide to join in the chase. Not knowing what else to do, as soon as I saw them start chasing us too, we just threw sodas everywhere. We started throwing bottles back at them as we cut into the first driveway we saw, right into some person's backyard. (Our traditional escape route when anybody was after us was to start going through yards.) So we run into this backyard far enough ahead of them - they are barely coming into the driveway when we get there - but in the back of the yard we're stopped dead!

There is a high fence and also this garage, but this garage is so old and creaky it looks like one of those abandoned buildings you see in Virginia City or some other ghost town. Half the siding was missing, it was leaning and it was just a terrible-looking wreck of an old garage and there was a rose trellis next to it, so I wasn't about to slow down. I started going up the trellis to get on the roof of the old garage. No sooner did I get up there, than the garage starts swaying on us, back and forth, and it's moving around all over the place. Bud is behind me and he starts to cry because he's getting scared, and I don't blame him and here come these guys pounding into the backyard and seeing us like a pack of hounds after a fox and I can see that they are going to be able to get my brother. He is not up high enough and this guy in the front is already getting ready to leap and grab Bud's ankles. So not knowing what else to do (I was on the end of the garage), I reached down and grabbed my brother's arm, and as in all emergencies you don't know where the strength comes from, it just seems to be there. I pull him up as hard as I can and he comes flying up, parallel with me, flying onto the roof of the garage and he hits the roof BOOM! The two of us start to head toward the back of the garage to jump off the other side, but these guys start to climb up this trellis as well. So they are in hot pursuit and we don't know what's going to happen, but as we start running across the roof, the whole garage starts moving back and forth, so we get to the end and jump off. The old garage collapses into the yard with a horrible sound. I don't know if there was a car in there or not, but if there was it was good-bye car. The whole damn thing caved in, which stopped everybody!

This lady was in the backyard by this time. She stops dead, these guys stop dead, and we are standing on the other side of this wreckage looking at them, not moving either. Before anybody can get going, I grab Bud and say, "come on let's keep on going." So over a fence we go, still hearing them chase us. I guess they came to their senses and realized "hey, they're getting away!" so they are kind of chasing us while we are running full blast through yards. We come to a fence about 4 feet high and on the other side we hear this vicious barking, but we are so panicked we don't even care. I try to go over like a hurdler going over a hurdle and my foot catches the top of the fence and knocks the whole damn fence down and we come crashing through, with fence flying all over the place. The dogs, two German shepherds, take off running. We scared the living Jesus out of them. Running straight through, we hear voices coming out of the house. "What the hell?" And we kept running down the driveway and through about 4 or 5 blocks of peoples' yards, over fences, under fences, through this, through that, knocking down anything that got in our way and heading north towards Soto Street. We followed the alley heading toward the bridge that went over the freeway and ran into Fud somewhere along that bridge and he just looks at us like "hey guys, what happened?" By this time we're kind of getting over it and it was starting to seem a little funny. Looking back, it sounds like a secondary comedy with the keystone cops in hot pursuit of somebody, or Laurel and Hardy or something, but it was rather exciting and it was typical of the kind of jams you get into when you're a kid, because like I said the streets were our playgrounds, crime meant nothing to us, if we could get away with it, we did it. We had absolutely no respect for law and order. What so ever.

Basically, we both kind of punched Fud out a little bit. We were really mad at him, but that's the way he was…he wasn't dumb; it was just things happened to him and he would get distracted at the wrong time. But it kind of made me realize that the three of us probably should stay out of organized crime. Because if that one caper was a typical example of our highly organized scheme to do things, I mean we were in the wrong line of business…let's stay straight, let's stay in school.

Anyway, it was an exciting little adventure and we were going to get all the soda we could drink and ended up running for our lives down the street. I sometimes chuckle as I think of what it must have looked like to those people who were watching from their porches as we ran by with soda bottles flying up in the air leaving this awful mess. Anyway, those were the days. Once you were out of the house, life was one big adventure for us. And now on with the story.

The twins continued their life of crime and my mom got use to them getting into one mess after another. One day the cops came to our door with the twins in hand. Both boys looked sick. They had tried to steal a car. Correction a jeep. Fud, being taller, sat at the wheel, while Bud pushed the pedals. They were stopped before they could do any harm but they got a stern warning from the police. Did it do any good? Nope.

One other adventure we had was the walk to the show. This was over the roller coaster hills, which took time, and we were impatient to get to the show. We all had our quarters and time was a wasting. Now we found out that about the time we would go to the show a slow train ran right past the playground and we would hop it and ride all the way to the City Terrace show. When we came out we did the same. We became pros at jumping freights. You ran along side and grabbed the ladder and pulled your legs up. The bridge over the tracks was built later and then we could walk to the Wabash or Brooklyn show. Twenty-five cents was all it cost for the full afternoon. Two movies and one cartoon. When the bridge was built it also opened up an access to another barrio. Not a friendly one. Brooklyn "Flips" and "Flats". This is important later on in the story.

CHAPTER SEVENTEEN: HOW WE WERE READY FOR ANYTHING

We all would walk to Lincoln Park swimming pool and I found I loved to swim. I was a fish. Still am. Everyone in the Gardens would catch the Sierra Vista bus on Lancaster and Soto to go downtown to the Goodwill store for our swimsuits. Yes, we did a lot of shopping there…all of us. This is how we got our wardrobes. How we were ready for anything.

Murchison Elementary was up from the lane to Little King's Chair and down the other side of the hill. In spring the hill was green and the wind would blow and flowers were all over. Carmen's store was located across from school and it would capture our pennies and Kits were our favorites. When I walked into school that first year I met for the first time a boy who took my breath away. He had dimples, no, I mean dimples, in both cheeks and he was small and hung out with the older boys. Yep, white tee shirt, jeans and a ducktail. He could whistle by just tucking his lower lip in. His name was David Martinez and joy! He lived only two units away. Things were looking up. He would walk home with me sometimes and just trade hits with me. Joy, joy. Yep, I was smitten. Only problem was Patsy Gonzales, green eyes and long brown hair, liked him too. If he walked her home he didn't trade hits. Later they would call him "Weasel." He lived next to Dory and she was my friend and watched him for me, sometimes. It depended whose friend she was for the week. Later in life Dory married him.

Now I started to meet more Mexicans and our group started changing. In the sixth grade I had a very nice teacher named Mr. McGarry. We learned to dance and soon everyone would go to my house after school to dance and socialize. Joe Martinez, later known as "Jo Jo," Isaac Mendoza, Joe Quintana, and Dickie Luna, all came over to slobber over my big sister Josie. She was only twelve and she looked like a young lady, shape and all. She was one of the prettiest girls in the project and now she knew it. She had tenth graders after her. We were still square and "Stranger in Paradise" was popular.

At night this boy named Richard Weidman would come over to see Josie and he brought David along. Could life be sweeter? We all would talk and it was the awkward age. You don't know what to say or where your voice is coming from. David would be cool. He kept combing his hair and whistling at the stars. It would be cold and they both would wear leather jackets. The smell still gets me. Soon a boy named Louie joined us. He was half-Filipino and half-Mexican. Richard was white with a Mexican attitude. Now Josie would go for walks, not me. I was scared. A handsome boy-man by the name of Frank Fairfield started coming over and I don't know if he was there to visit my mom, who was very pretty, or Josie. He was eighteen and he was Mexican-mix. My mom would get all fluttery when he was there. He would joke with her and I think he was confused. Scarlet had them all wrapped around her finger.

We began to hear other music. It was rhythm and blues. "Loudy Miss Cloudy" and "One Mint Julep." I went into my twelfth year learning to dance and Pachuca hop was in. Now we spent nights out in my front yard with the guys and girls we had come to know. Things were beginning to change. We hung out with all Mexicans and gone were the children's games. We were meeting all the girls in the Gardens and now our group hung out on the lane singing and joking. The guys hung out with us but sat separate on the hill behind us. Lolly Molina, Beatrice Lopez and I were the *chavalitas* of the group. No one took us seriously. We were tolerated. Jolly, Rosemary, Sally and Martha Rocha were the older girls of thirteen/fourteen. We were all changing and no one knew this. Older brothers now were looking at us with a different look. It might have helped that most of the girls were stuffing their little bras with scarves and tissues. No Jolly and Rosemary, I won't tell.

Now came the sad time of graduation from Murchison and the entrance into Lincoln High School. There was no junior high for us. I don't think the school board thought that we would stay in school long enough to warrant a junior high. I will always remember getting a bus pass and waiting with the big kids for the bus to this new adventure I thought I was prepared for. We all went shopping at our favorite store, Goodwill, and so I had new clothes. I was still young in mind and wore dresses to school because pants were not allowed. The older girls wore nylon blouses and full skirts. The Pachucas wore tight skirts and sweaters two sizes too small with high socks and white teardrop shoes. Corduroy jackets with scarves in their hair. I like it. The bus would pick us up in front of Murchison and you give a smart look at the little children that were hurrying into the elementary school. Yes, I was a pre-teen on my way to high school. I now wore black ballerina shoes with no socks and short poodle hairdo - this was in - or the Italian boy hair cut. UGH!

I remember the first time pulling up at Lincoln and thinking it was as big as the project. We were let out at the front gate and this was so huge. Long stairs spread out from the opening and went in three directions. To the left the Auditorium. To the right the C Building and up more stairs the Main Building. The anxiety intensified. We were shuffled like cattle into the Auditorium and given a rundown on where our homerooms were. Someone goofed and I was put into the famous "tracking" of smart kids. I could keep up I guess but they had put all my friends in another group and they looked like they were having fun. They were hanging out. I guess I could have pulled it off but when we pulled up at Lincoln I remember thinking how big it was and as we climbed the stairs to our classes the older kids would snicker. I thought it was because we were so young and when I woke up I realized it was because we were from the projects. I hung out with the quote "good kids" and our group was the dorks. It became clear that we were being snubbed. Our clothes were nothing compared to the Anglo's matching outfits. Even at its best, Goodwill could only do so much. No one liked us. Teachers were downright rude. The girls vice, Miss "Looney Tunes" was a basket case and called us all chick-a-dees. She is the destroyer of many of her student's lives. I hope she realizes this.

CHAPTER EIGHTEEN: SADIE HAWKINS DANCE

I left my dorky friends and pulled more toward the older girls and because I was Josie's sister, they let Lolly and me hang around with them at school. At lunch we had our own spot. I'll say this much for these older girls. They didn't match the clothes in cost but they had class and soon all the guys were around our lunch spot. This brought the wrath of the Anglo girls because their boyfriends were hanging around with their tongues hanging out. The guys were now "Hazard" and started staking claims to the girls. Our group of girls became the Eastside girls. My first dance was a disaster. It was called the Sadie Hawkins Day Dance and all the girls invited a boy. I asked Marcello, cute but stupid. In order for our friends to get the money for the tickets we had to sell popcorn in the Gardens. I think we watched too many Judy and Mickey movies. Jolly and Josie would walk down the lanes and sing "popcorn, popcorn, popcorn," the words so sweet that I repeat, "you'll adore it." We sold it for five cents a bag and that's how we got our money. I was still a small thin girl and sort of funny looking. Well, I was only twelve. The night of the dance we were all excited and everyone borrowed clothes and as my date was at the front door, my skirt was coming in the back door. Junior answered the door and didn't like Marcello so he closed the door. I was screaming. Mom was trying to keep me calm. I wore a white nylon blouse and gray and black downward striped skirt with a tie at the waist. Ballerina shoes completed the outfit and a little Avon Wild Rose and I was ready. For once my hair came out nice. Don't forget we had no hairspray then. I remember "Hold Me" was playing on the radio in the front room; it was still a nice time to be alive.

The girls had arranged to walk together to the dance. It was far to Lincoln High and we had to walk through the park. It was beautiful. Stars shone and the night had flowers in the air. I don't remember too much about the dance itself, because I was getting ready for that first kiss. All I could think about was how I must remember to put my face to the side and that I must close my eyes. Well, this is the way it was done in the movies. As we all walked home I knew that as soon as we reached the park the kissing would start. My heart was racing and I felt faint. Could I do it? Yes, I was ready. He got my hand and the stars were a little brighter. Now he put his arm around me. All the older ones smiled and were getting a kick out of it. The girls knew I had never been kissed. What's this? A car drives up and Marcello's mother says, "get in the car young man." He left me there. All the girls and their boyfriends were sympathetic and I was crushed. He was never allowed on the lane again. He slinked around school after that and started hanging around with the dorks. Well that's what he was.

CHAPTER NINETEEN: FIRST KISS

The girls tolerated us or rather until the famous incident with the green and white polka dot swimsuit. It was a two-piece. I had bought the suit the year before at Goodwill and in one year, without my permission, I had gone from nothing to thirty-four and what was once a child's two piece suit was now a bikini. Well I get into the pool at Lincoln Park and I'm still a child mentally and all the guys were trying to dunk me. Yes, they would swing me way up in the air and down into the water. I guess they were trying to get my top to fall off. Thank God it didn't. I was having a great time and couldn't understand why Josie and the girls were glaring at me. Hey, the Aragon's (the jocks) offered us a ride home with me in the front. When we got home Josie pushed right past me and had a whispered conversation with Mom. She sends me upstairs to put on the suit. I come down and she sends me back up to change. Gave her the suit and she burnt it. No more football and no more going without a bra. I hated them. I wondered how she knew I didn't have one on. Dumb? Yes.

We started having dances at Lincoln Park on Wednesday nights after our club meeting. We were the revellers and our meetings were five minutes and three hours of dancing. As we would walk to the park for our meetings we would have a chain. First Josie and I would stop for Lolly and Beatrice who lived in the same unit. Then next would be Rosemary (Moe), when she didn't walk with her boyfriend Art. On to Jolly's who would sneak her brother Frankie's records out under her sweater. This was hard because they were seventy-eights and breakable. He always would come later to the dance and yell at us. He had the best records in the Gardens. "Rock Me Baby" and "I Cried" were just a few. The lights were always low and the park smelled of eucalyptus trees. Lolly and I were kept around for fun as we tried to act grown up. Beatrice was our age but she had two brothers, B.B. and Carlos, so she acted like she was above us in the chain of age.

We made tuna sandwiches in the kitchen and sold them at a loss for our activities. This included snow trips. We would rent a truck through the park and everyone paid to go. We found we could do this for all kinds of trips. Who needed dads for a wonderful day up in Angeles Crest Mountains or the beach? Beach parties were at night and it was a wondrous time. Everyone paired up. This is when I wanted a boyfriend. I turned thirteen and this older brother of my friend, Bobby Valdez, asked me to dance at the after meeting of our club. Lights low, leather jacket.

His name was Tony Valdez and he was from little Hazard. This was across Soto Street and the guys from little Hazard were part of our group. He asked me to go for a walk with him. He didn't give me time to think about it. I went as if I was walking on a cloud. We stopped by the pool and he pulled me gently to him and gave me my first kiss. It was wonderful. I felt like I was in a movie. He was the sweetest person and gentle, which I didn't expect. I'm so glad he was around at that time of my life. We kissed some more and he asked me to hang around with him. I said yes and he gave me his jacket to wear. We walked back to the dance and everyone was shocked. I found I liked to kiss and we danced and it was with two hands. His on my waist, mine on his shoulders. He walked me home and we would talk on the phone for hours and he would walk me to class at school and home after school.

I was starting to change and I started hanging around with another group from the Gardens. At the time we were forming there was another group, actually two other groups, forming. One group was more my age, Little Mary, Rosie, Tito, Gloria and Cathy. I joined them. They were more into being from Hazard. Later some of the older girls followed. There was this other group of girls that claimed to be from Hazard too. One of the leaders was this girl called "Rattler," later known as Bernie. What a pain they were. The blacks had a singing group called the "Sparrows" and they would sing to us every time they saw us walking. "Hey Senoritas" was the name of the song. They were great and everyone liked them. We sang on the lane and everyone said we sang like blacks and our voices matched perfect. We would stay on the lane until ten at night and this was when I was thirteen. The office was our second hangout. When we wanted to get away from the guys, we would hang out at the flagpole. Sometimes some of the guys would come down there but this was only when they liked one of us. I started to dress like them and soon I was the girl with the shaved eyebrows and short skirt. Hair high (stacked) with a tail, high socks and teardrops shoes. We hung out at the office and when Jolly and Moe were mad because we were Pachucas, they left the lane. Now it was our group with a few of the older girls. The other group was "Green Eyes" - "Nordella", Bernie and Joker. Joker was huge.

We still would go to the meetings at Lincoln Park and the dances turned out to be our chance to learn to smoke - our home base. Now I had gone around with Tony for a month and a half and at that age it is forever. Richard (Monko) and Freddie had entered the service, Korea. He came home on leave and I guess I had grown up because he cornered me at the lane and started kissing me. As I said, I liked to kiss. I was so confused because at that time if you were going around you didn't cheat. I went home and when Tony called, I broke up. Not that I thought I would go with Monko, but because I found I didn't know what I wanted. Monko and I wrote, along with half the girls in the Gardens, while he was in the service. Freddie was going with Jolly. Hands off. Now I, along with the rest of the group, was wearing jeans and concha belts. No one messed with us. When we walked into Lincoln now the smart asses were scared and no one snickered at us. School was just a place to go during the day to see our friends. We had our place to hang out and sad to say, Josie was over on the other side with Rosemary, Sally, Lulu and Jolly. Lolly was with us until the famous fight. That came about because of me. Strange, huh?

CHAPTER TWENTY: THE FAMOUS FIGHT

As I said, there was another group of girls saying they were from Hazard and we tolerated them. One of the girls, "Green Eyes," was going around with the cutest boy named Joe Hernandez. Well, he started calling me and soon he came over to see me. A mad Green Eyes was sending me threats. Joe asked me to go around with him and I said yes. This did it. She and her friends were going to beat me up after school and the girls said, oh, no you don't. Soon it was all over school and when school ended we all went home and changed into jeans. I was still small and thin, but a person has to do what she has to do. I was scared but I wouldn't let anyone know it. We all met at the lane and I remember even Jolly was there. No Rosemary, Lulu or Sally, this was the splitting of the group. Little Mary's mom was in labor and yet she still came. Tommy was born that day. Then they showed up. Joker looked big and she had singled me out. I had my heart in my throat. As we faced each other, the older girls from Hazard, German, Sukey and some other girls, came to watch. The guys were on the hill and my boyfriend Joe (Clown) was not there. I think all the Gardens were there. A yell and the fight began. All I remember is Joker coming at me and like a trapped animal I struck out. I jumped on her and she fell back. Her head hit the corner of a step and I just sat on her hitting her head on the step.

I think I went crazy. Next thing I knew someone yelled cops or rather "La Juda." We all ran home but Joker just sat there. I was only home five minutes and the cops came to my door for Josie and me. They took us down to Hollenbeck Police Station and all the girls were there. All our mothers were calling and we all began a long record. We were sent home with a warning, first offense. When I got home Clown was there and boy was he proud of me. He told me everyone was talking about the way I hit Joker. Guess who didn't have to fight again? I made my name that day and we became the only girls from Hazard. We had a different walk and a different talk but when we were alone we acted like all teenagers and cracked up at silly things. We all got grounded for a while, but there were too many kids to keep track of. Moms were tired and they forgot. Clown would come over every night and we would walk and talk. We also made out. I think we grew very close and maybe I was afraid but I broke up with him after a few months. He got drunk and everyone said, "Look what you are doing to him." He put my name on his arm, you know, like a home tattoo, and back I went with him. I did like him. I actually grew up with him. We went together for a long time. We also went through his knee surgery and my eye surgery.

I would walk with the girls to school every morning and if we made it to third period we were doing good. We would smoke on the way to school and hang out first in the park and then we would, of course, have to hang out at Hams. This was a soda shop across from Lincoln and it was ours. Everyone hung out there. We would order sodas and play records on the Jukebox. "Unchained Melody" and "Lovely Dove" were Number One and "Oh What A Dream" came close. We would walk into Lincoln when we wanted to and no one said anything. We just ditched. If we missed a whole day, the one with the best handwriting would write the excuse. I was now in the group I belonged in. The mess-ups. There were smart kids in this class but they were the pachucos. Rocky, Alfred and Joe Chico were in this class and we all had fun. Rocky was an Italian and his older brother, Luis Eugino, dated Josie. Actually, he took her to his prom. They called him "Gook" and Rocky was "Little Gook". Rocky was cute with the blackest eyes I have ever seen; I guess if he had been older I would have dated him. He was one of the younger boys from little Hazard. I don't know why I didn't date boys my own age, probably because they couldn't stay out as late as I could and they couldn't date. I had fun with them in class and Clown was the video monitor and would come to our class to show films and I would sit in the back with him. Teachers didn't notice. We would talk and have fun while the rest of the class learned. How square.

If we wanted to get out of class you could catch the wastebasket on fire and the teacher would let you out. We did this a few times in Social Studies. English. If we set the teachers hair and combed it out we got an A for the day. Sad but true. We had teachers with blue wigs and others with no hair. One teacher was called Madame Fi Fi. These were the kind of teachers we had.

CHAPTER TWENTY-ONE: JIVING

Junior was protected because he was our brother but he would get mad when he walked the main hall and all the guys would say "Hey, professor." He would walk past with his nose up in the air. Little Mary and Rosie would chase him for a kiss. He would run from them and get to his special class for eye-impaired. He also was a genius and was a straight A student. This brings to mind one of the most embarrassing times of my life and to my shame, one of my brother's too. I was in fourth period with all my friends and in comes' Junior with a summons from Miss Hill. She was my English teacher and a bitch. She enjoyed herself at other's expense. Well, he comes in and my teacher calls me up and gives me the summons. I go to walk with my brother and he takes off. I tried to catch him but he is mad and I will not run. When I get to Miss. Hill's room he is already seated. She proceeds to yell at me in front of my brother and his friends and tell me she knows my type and I will be pregnant by the time I am sixteen. She and the school were wasting their time by trying to educate me. "Get out!" she yelled and I could see my brother slink down in his chair. I gave her a look that said I hate you and she knew it. I didn't tell her to go to hell because my brother was there. To this day I despise her. I left that classroom and thought to myself forget this shit. I never went back to her class. She sent me spinning on a rebellious path and I'm only glad I didn't do more harm to myself. I really became a problem then. We use to walk down the hallways and shoot the girls in front of us on the butt with a water gun. Some of those "matching outfits." They were too scared to say anything. We would push some and they wouldn't fight back. We would crack up. We would stay out of class and spend the time in the restroom smoking and talking. "

One way we would entertain ourselves was to tattoo our hands, fingers, face and legs. Not big tattoos like animals or things but letters, crosses, or dots. We would spend our PE time using India ink. We would use a needle with string wrapped around near the point, dip it in the ink and puncture our skin. After a few days you peeled off the scab and there it was. We all had tattoos and I have taken some off but most cannot be removed. Embarrassing at dinners or talking when you wave your hand or use it to eat and someone notices. I went for a medical exam recently for arthritis and Dr. Howe looked at my hand and said, "You were in a gang?" I think she was floored. You are marked for life and all the girls from our group put an "H" in the inside of their ring finger. This I think we all cover with a ring. Nowadays the kind of rings we used to only dream of.

We used to put our boyfriend's names or initials on our legs and then we ran into problems because we were always breaking up. All the girls were *Paloma Negras* (Black Doves) and couldn't be kept. We all liked to date and date more than one guy. We would see how many guys we could mess around with. In those days messing around was just kissing and most girls held onto their virginity because if you got pregnant, you were a *puta* or you got married. We only had one girl get married that way when we were only fourteen. The rest of the girls held tight until they were sixteen or seventeen, which at that time was old in East Los Angeles. Then we would have the big wedding, with the white dress and all in the church with ten to fifteen couples in the wedding. People just have to understand that at that time if you were not married and a mother by the time you were sixteen or seventeen, there was something wrong with you.

You can see how the pattern was kept going by listening to Rose Lopez, President of P.I.C.A. (Parents Involved in Community Action). The scenario, in her words, goes like this: A child has a family made up of a young mother and father. The father doesn't finish school so he has a minimal job and he sees some of these friends going out and having fun, driving a new car. The mother and father had to get married in the first place, and so started the family. They never got the chance to grow up. Now the child grows up and sees his mother and father fighting and drinking because they are so miserable and he says this will not happen to me. I love my girl and if she gets pregnant

We will get married and I will take care of her. Now he starts hanging around with the guys and girls and then he meets the <u>one</u> and she gets pregnant will marry her and they will live happily ever after. Now he starts to hang out with the guys and the pattern starts all over again. We must stop the pattern and also explain to girls that they don't have to prove they love their guys by having their babies. Nowadays the guys don't marry the girls anyway so think before you give in. I just can't help it. I see it all the time and you see young girls carrying babies. I hope they get a second chance and finish school at least. I support the teenage pregnancy programs in high school. Just on a different campus so as not to give the other girls the idea that babies are cute, and boy, that "Chavala" sure loves her "Vato". I got married at eighteen and that was old. All my friends had been married a couple of years and had kids. I saw too much to fall for that line.

CHAPTER TWENTY-TWO: THE COUSINS

During this time my Aunt Flora decided that my cousins should get together with us and become friends. Enter Terry. Now she was a spoiled brat and when they brought her over it was a trip for us. She was from, or rather hung out, with the girls from "Flats" and she went to Sacred Heart Catholic School along with my cousin Dolly. She remembers coming to my house when I made my Confirmation and we clicked. We would go to her house and stay on weekends or she would stay with us. While she was in the Gardens she captured many hearts and went around with Frankie. Then when we were at her house she went steady with Brother from Flats. I asked her why she went with both and she said she felt sorry for them. I would repeat the pattern later on. When we stayed at her house we would go to the dances at Lords. This was the favorite hangout for all East Los Angeles. The guys were all fine and could dance everything. All the guys were older so of course we all lied about our ages. Josie and Terry were always 17 or 18. They would get mad at me because when the guys asked how old I was, I would say 13 or 14 and they would say, "but they said you all were older". Then I would tell them they were a year older so figure it out. The girls would get mad.

I still remember Flora making a thousand pies and freezing them in the freezer. Terry's father was real quiet and her sister Kitty and brother Larry were just babies and seemed like shadows. Bobby and Billy were young married people then and didn't scare Terry as much as they did earlier. Dolly would spy on us and if she saw us smoking she would blackmail us into taking her somewhere. A few years difference matters at that age. She was a pain. When we were at Lords we would run into that strange girl Bernice who hung around with Green-Eyes and she would be friendly. We all couldn't make up our minds about her.

Around this time Tutie (Martha), another cousin (Flora's sister Martha's daughter) had her sixteenth birthday party and we got to be there. We were punks and Martha was sophisticated and the guys who were at her party were from Roosevelt and Garfield High Schools. Well, we were in our glory. All that meat. Tutie did not want us at her party but Martha and Flora made her invite us. Frances, Tutie's younger sister, was Dolly's age and too young to be there. Ha, ha!

Here we go and even though Tutie had said not to bother the guys, this was a once in a lifetime chance for us. We had our make-up and we tried to dress older. We were in the front yard right in the middle of the guys and we made pests of ourselves. I know this is hard to imagine knowing how sophisticated we were. As we let up and tried to talk to the guys they must have thought we were stupid brats. We asked them for a cigarette and they said, "sure here you go". We lit up and then they started to laugh and with all dignity we asked them, "What was so funny?" They said they had given us Spanish fly and now they would just wait. Well we all had heard stories about Spanish fly and off we ran to Tutie's room and we hid and shook. We kept asking each other if we felt anything. Terry said she had heard of a girl using a coke bottle because she was crazy with Spanish fly. We spent the whole party in Tutie's room. "Now we went to parties every weekend and all the parties had blue lights and the guys would be wearing leather jackets. They had Three Flowers on their hair and the combined smell would make you fall in love. At least for the evening. If you were going around with someone you wore his jacket and just danced with him. For me it was Clown. When they would play "I" or "My Girl Awaits Me," we would dance. Then your boyfriend would walk you home and you would kiss on the way. In the Gardens you would walk down the lanes and they had benches along the walk where you could stop and talk or just fool around. Most of the time we would walk with Josie and whoever her boyfriend was at that time, and talk. No one checked to see what time we got home but mom always gave us a deadline and if we took advantage of it and she caught us, we would get grounded for a few days. This is where the respect came in. Mom was by herself and now we were taller than she was and yet we never said, "No, I'm not staying in." We could have walked all over her, but we didn't. She still held the reins and we didn't argue.

I remember one day I was at school and we all were at lunch. Into the schoolyard walks Tony Valdez, my first boyfriend, all bloody and beaten up. He walks up to me and says, "Nellie, I never talked about you, I swear." I knew that. We were friends. Now come the guys from Hazard and I find out Joe has gotten into a fight with Tony using me as an excuse. I knew this was bogus. I break up with him. Now Joe is mad because he thinks I still like Tony. He didn't get it. After a while we make up and go back together for the third time. I think we were getting a little serious then. Our making out was changing and he had his knee surgery and I went across town to be with him. He was with me for my eye surgery and stayed with me while I wore a patch over my eye. A lot of jokes went on that he had given me a black eye but he never touched me. Once more I found myself getting too involved and so I broke up for the last time. He went around with Judy from Rosehill and they stayed together for a long time.

CHAPTER TWENTY-THREE: THREE STRIKES AND YOU'RE OUT

At Lincoln High School they had what they call "white cards" that were in the girl's Vice Office. When you were bad, they gave you a card and for, say a month; you couldn't go to assemblies or anything special at school. Ohhh! So while all the good kids went to boring assemblies we would all meet in ding-a-lings office and mess around. They would even let us go together to the restroom where we lit up and spent an enjoyable hour. I broke the record at Lincoln when I was given a "blue card." Only boys got them. I was the first girl. Well, I was finally first at something. This came about when Rocky and Joe Chico sent me a note in Mr. Carr's math class. Does he get them? No, just me. Well, he shakes me by my leather jacket (can't remember whose it was) and sends me to Mrs. dingalings. I already had four white cards, so she gives me a blue. Instead of being ashamed I was proud. Josie was mad and she and Jolly, Sally, Rosemary and Lulu stayed completely away from us. Little Mary, Tito, Rosie and Gloria still were together. Now the drinking started to enter our stupid heads. White Port and lemon juice, it only cost seventy-five cents and twenty-five cents a lemon.

During these times we would get drunk and then go to Lincoln Park and look for girls to jump. They were what we called "Patties," Whites. We would take their clothes or just embarrass them. Little Mary always got after one of the younger girls. This was usually Gloria because she would not fight back. Then she would apologize and we would all be okay. Just a few years ago we would ride the merry-go-round as little girls and now we jumped on without paying. The owner, a bald man with green eyes, would be smoking and yell at us. We would jump off and run up the hill laughing. Next our boyfriends would join us and we would sit on the hill watching everyone to make sure they were ours. Next we would all make-out. Joe would walk me home.

When we walked home from school, it was a time to look for things to do. We jumped the trolley that ran in front of the school for a ride who knows where. The trolley had wood chairs and the windows were huge. We sat in the back and hung out the windows. One day, Joe and I, Josie and Johnny Avila, and I don't remember who else, were walking home from school and we passed the General Hospital. Across the street, Joe remembers, there was morgue. He said, "Let's go in" and we say, "No, it has dead people." He called us chicken and that was all we needed. We got in through the back window and people's bodies were hanging all over the room. An arm here and a leg there. I almost threw up. They had bodies just laying there in the open, not in coffins but on gurneys. It was awful and I remember looking at this one man's eyes and thinking he was just alive and now look at him. This began the realization of mortal beings. I started to get chills and we left. I remember having nightmares for a long time. I will not say the jokes that the guys were saying because it was stupid. I will never give my body to science. No one watches you, or rather everyone sees you. Donate parts but not the whole body.

Joe would always try to get rides so we could cruise, but it was because of Josie that we would get rides. All the guys would come down in cars for Josie and I guess she felt it was good having us with her. I remember one guy named "Debussy", that was his whole name, or "Tweety" from Alpine. His first name was Joe. He took his father's Model A and we went for a long ride in it. We also rode in a hearse and the car had shades.

Josie was mad about Johnny Avila and he and Joe were friends. We four would sit by my house on some benches that were in a square. When Joe was not with the guys he was smart, sensitive. I used to sing for him and he would swing me on a gate. When I met his mother and father, I found them to be very quiet and nice. Vera liked me and when Joe had his surgery, I went to his house to see him. He was glad but I was bashful. He lived next to Hazard Park on Norfolk. I think we were both too young for what was happening and I'm glad we didn't do anything. We both changed later as we grew up. Well, you'll see later.

On the way to school we would all meet at the flagpole in front of the office of the Project. We would all walk up to Venegas' store where little Mary's father had an account. She would go in and get lettuce, lunchmeat, bread and a pack of Lucky's, too. Now we would walk to the park, sometimes Hazard Park or Lincoln Park, and have a picnic. Then of course we would spend another hour at Hams smoking and drinking cokes; the guys would join us or hang out on the corner. Always close. We would get into school when we felt like it. That's okay; we still passed to the next grade. We had all F's and still passed. Heck, this school stuff was great. One day we were walking behind Camille. She lived in the Gardens but was not one of us. She walked with a swing and we found out some of the guys from Hazard were going down her house to see her. Lolly shot her on the butt with the famous water gun. She kept walking so she shot her again. We were cracking up. She turns and pushes Lolly. Well, they have a push and shove and a fight is to be held after school in Lincoln Park. Comes the hour and she shows up, which surprised us. They fight and Lolly whipped ass. Now we laughed. I told her she was mine and I would get her the next day. Next day I'm called into the girl's Vice Office and a policeman is there with Camille crying. Oh no! They talk about me as if I'm not there and they kick me out of Lincoln. No one else, just me. And where do they send me? To Hollenbeck Junior High School. This is located right in the middle of enemy territory - "Flats." Now what do I do?

CHAPTER TWENTY-FOUR: ACT TOUGH

I was going around with a guy named Leroy and he was from the Brooklyn Flips. They got along with Flats and Hazard. His sister was in our group but hung around with Josie and that group. Her name was Velma. I was so shook up I couldn't sleep the night before I was to start school. Would I get jumped? Would I know anyone? I had to act tough or I would get jumped.

Next morning I got off the bus and walked up sixth to the front of the school. All the little Dukes from Flats were lined up and I had to pass them. They said "Mama Hazard" and a few choice words and as I passed they pushed me. I still don't know how they knew I was coming. I kept going and gave them the meanest look I could manage. I think I dreaded more entering the school where the girls would be. "Blinky" a voice yells out and who comes running at me but that weirdo Bernice. I was never so glad to see anyone in my life. Her cousin Edna and some girls followed her from Flats. Bless you; bless you, I thought. I found Bernie to be one of my closest friends and we got into more trouble because we are both rascals. We were in detention together and we made the great escape from Hollenbeck that changed my life completely.

When I took Bernie home with me, she only lived a few units away, she brought her little green plastic radio and we would listen to Harland Hancock. He played nothing but Rhythm and Blues. There were two types of music out then, White and our R&B. All the Black songs were sung by Whites for Whites, and there were two stations. So there was one station for us and one for the Whites. They missed a lot of good music.

When Josie came home from school she walked in and took one look at Bernie and yelled "Mom, what is she doing here?" Mom took her into the kitchen and told her to shut up; this was my friend from Hollenbeck. She came back in and ignored us. Bernie just pretended everything was fine. Soon Josie and Bernie were best friends and I was the third. Josie was still at Lincoln so it was just Bernie and I who walked to school together. Thank God the bridge was built going over the freeway so Bernie and I could go down side streets to school. I enjoyed Hollenbeck and made many friends. Except the Little Dukes. The irony of it was we (the girls) would go out with their older brothers. One day as I was going down the hall to class with my new friends Patsy and Vickie, these punks came up behind us and started pushing me calling me names. "La Hazard Mama," said huero. He was big and stupid. He kept pushing me and when I turned he was ready to hit me. Fight, fight, yelled everyone. A crowd was soon formed and he pushed me and the fight was on. I hit, he hit and just when I thought no one cared, a guy named Gitano came up and said, "Hit a guy." I was doing okay but was I glad to see him. Huero fell down the stairs and anyone looking up only saw me so from that time on I never had to fight again at Hollenbeck. I hardly knew Gitano but he was class. He was from State and never tried to go out with me. We stayed friends.

Now for the great getaway. Bernie, Molly and I were in school and it was lunchtime. Outside the fence was Bernie's cousin Edna. She was from New York, too, and her last name was Fernandez. Well she is with some guys and she says come on out and play. How can we? The teacher is walking back and forth where the gate is. Of course there is the gate next to the stairs in the side yard. Off we go and any commando would be proud of the way we snuck around. We ran, stopped, ran, and stopped. When we rounded the corner near the gate we made a dash for the stairs. Made it. "Go girls!" the girls yelled. The teacher turns and looks at us and starts to blow her whistle. We jump the gate and keep running with all the girls at the fence yelling, "Go, go!" down Mott Street to Fourth. We felt pretty cocky. We went in to Henna's, a version of Hams, and lit up a cigarette. Henna is yelling "Buy, buy!" She is Chinese and is she mean. We order sodas and Edna is already there with her friends. We sit in a booth and who should pull up but Mrs. McDonald, the girls' Vice at Hollenbeck. The Principal is with her. Bernie and I drop to the floor under the table and Edna and her friends hide us. Henna says, "There they are." She had the first smile I ever saw on her face. They take us out like criminals and put us in the back seat. We stuff the pack of cigarettes down the seat and back we go to school.

When we get back to school a strange thing happened. Mrs. McDonald looks at us and says "Why?" No one had asked that before. Not mad just confused. I don't know but it sort of starts you thinking. I liked being in school so why did I do it? Bernie and I are being ourselves looking like we don't care and because I was younger, Mrs. McDonald says Bernie is a bad influence and sends her to Ramona, better known as Enchandia, a school for girls. Bernie gives me this look that says it's okay and the Principal gives us back the cigarettes he got from his back seat. Bernie is a big hero and Josie is at home acting like my mom when the Principal calls. I got off light. A meeting was set up for my counselor and me. This was to change my life and thank God for the chance I was given.

Later that day we take Josie with us to the park and all the girls put their money together for our White Port and we all take a swig. Josie takes the bottle from me and cries "Nellie, think of Mama". Sure whatever. Then Josie is teased into taking a drink and after that I would be the one pleading for her to remember Mama. She was an alcoholic and could never take just one drink. She was the one that got sloppy and she now escaped into the bottle. I had to stay with her at all times when we were out to make sure I provided her with safety. Since she was so pretty, guys took advantage of her and girls wanted to beat her up. That's why I had to stay at her side. I used to want to beat her when she would use her smart mouth. She would smile this side smirk and you would want to smack her. I don't care who you were.

We still met almost every night at the lane or the flagpole and one time the guys came over to us and said, "You girls are from Hazard and we don't want you going out with anyone else. You stop bringing Vatos down here." Yeah, right. Some of the girls took them serious and some didn't. Namely us. How could you take them serious when they were so high on drugs that most of the time they didn't even know their names. Were we to choose from this large assortment our soul mates?

CHAPTER TWENTY-FIVE: NOT GETTING STUCK IN THE GARDENS

Bernie, Josie and Mary along with her cousin Big Mary, and me, said you know, there must be something over the hill and we need to find out what. We went over the hill (Lancaster) to Soto and started walking to Whittier Boulevard where we knew people from all over hung out. One time we walked all the way to Little Caesars which was on Olympic and Soto. We never worried about rides home because we would either meet someone we knew or they knew - a mutual friend. Sometimes they just talked right and then we got rides with them. Soon they were coming to the Gardens to pick us up. One thing became clear to us; we were not going to get stuck in the Gardens. There was a whole new world out there. East Los Angeles. Rows and rows of Chicano guys. In the projects by now, most of the guys were on the needle and didn't make much sense. They would get up at the crack of dawn and steal milk from the steps of the people's homes and then sell it to get their fix. They would steal anything not nailed down or they were cool dealers. Once I was walking to the store and German comes up to me and starts to walk with me. He is sucking on an ice cream stick and says "Hey Nellie, did you know the Chinese would die for a bowl of rice?" "Oh Yeah?" I would say. "Hey Nellie, did you know that the Chinese would die for a bowl of rice?" over and over he would repeat himself. His older brother Choncla was my hero. He was a hype, but he was cool. He loved my singing because I could scat. "My Little Red Top" was his favorite. He would sit with me at the park on the lane or anywhere else and have me sing it over and over. No one dared touch me. Everyone was afraid of him.

Bernie and I would still walk to Soto street where she caught the bus and I met Vicky. While walking Bernie and I spotted this house for rent right on Soto Street, 805 N. Soto Street. Perfect. All the cars cruised by it. It was big and had two palm trees in the front yard, big windows and a porch. We got the number and Mom called and I remember it was $150 a month, a lot at that time. Well Josie and I swear to give up everything if she will just move us. The girls all begged knowing we could sit out on the porch and watch all the cars go by. Mom agrees and calls the landlord. We got it. When we moved it was with the help of our friends and mainly Big Eddie. His last name was Gonzales and he was like a brother to Bernie and me and was madly in love with Josie. Eddie. I remember when I met him. I was walking from Bernie's unit to ours when down the lane Gilbert Martinez came skating, a boy I knew from school. He was my age so he was still a chavalo. He was with two other guys and stopped to talk to me. I talked to him because you could see in his eyes if I didn't he would die. He introduced me to Ernie Madrid and Eddie. Gilbert was small built and Ernie was medium and Eddie was huge. Eddie was like a big bear. Well they follow me home and I introduced them to Josie. They couldn't talk. Bernie shows up and now they are dumbstruck. They almost did cartwheels to entertain us. Mom loved Eddie and he did many things to make our lives easier.

Eddie's father owned a construction company and all Eddie's brothers and dad worked constantly. Eddie would sometimes get his father's car and take my mom, of course this included Josie, shopping or to the show. Gilbert, Ernie, and Eddie became part of our family. Gilbert's family owned a store and he was in the R.O.T.C.

along with my brother Junior. Junior would ignore him when he came over. They couldn't stand each other.

CHAPTER TWENTY-SIX: LAST TIME CRUISIN' IN THE GARDENS

We six had many adventures and just to recall a few, one night Josie, Bernie and I were sitting on my front steps in the Gardens when up pulls Eddie, Gilbert, and Ernie. "Come on, let's go cruising," they shout. "Sure, let's go." In we pile and then we cruise all over. When we got home they let us know they had hotwired it. After that we checked to make sure they had a key for whatever car they showed up in. The six of us would walk to the show and we all remained friends for many years. It was funny because they had money and they knew we didn't so they would always take us to eat. Eddie would buy Josie whatever she wanted. The Cup was our favorite hangout on Wabash and Soto. It was by chance that when we moved it would be right up the street from The Cup. When guys would come to see us on Soto we would mention the food at The Cup and they would take us to eat. Not just Bernie, Josie and me, but all the girls. They had pastrami and malts that were out of this world. We would listen to music on the jukebox. "Roll With Me Henry" and "Sixteen Tons" were popular. "Death of an Angel" was out and I remember they took it off the radio because it was what they called a depression song. "Work With Me Annie" and "Annie IIad A Baby" were taken off too because Paul Coates, on his T.V.

show, said it was the teenager's downfall. We didn't know what the words meant. Dumb. When this great reporter presented this special, he had this fat Anglo whom was a wonabe swinging back and forth to the music.

We knew what a phony he was because just weeks before he had come to the gardens and at a hotdog stand that no one hung out at, he filmed all of us dancing and presented Rudy Padilla, the student body president, as a gang member dancing. He asked us to dance and bought sodas. Buy us a soda and will follow you anywhere.

While we lived on Soto, my brothers, Bud and Fud, made shoe shine boxes and would go out on Brooklyn to the bars and stand outside the bars to shine shoes. They got their money this way. This is when they learned to sing Mexican songs and soon they picked up the guitar. Fud sang Javier Solis songs that were played in the bars then. He can't speak Spanish but he can sing it. Those boys would be out there until one or two in the morning. They were just babies at that time. Then they started tasting the bad life and they liked it. Bud started wearing his hair slicked down with some of it straight out in the front. They started running with a guy named Little Johnny and next thing I know they are always in trouble.

They started running away from home and we would have to find them. We had all our friends looking for them and even had the guys from the "Avenues" running after them.

Talk about an image breaker. Sonny (who becomes my husband) and his friends had gone to pick me up at Roosevelt and as we would cruise the school I would see my little brother, Fud, with some friends. He had been missing for three days and was only eleven or twelve. "Stop!" I yell. "Catch him," I say. These cool guys jump out of the car and chase him over fences and down alleys and finally they come back to the car breathing hard. As we drive around the school in Sonny's '56 Chevy the guys try to recapture the "cool look" but it is too late. Everyone saw them. Fud got picked up by the cops later that day and returned home until the next time. Bud stayed home. He had a dog named Red and that was all he needed…Red and Bud…a team.

When we would walk to school, Vickie and I would argue over who's hair was longer or rather who's tail was longer. You had this high, curly, hairdo with a straight tail in the back. Danny Alarcon lived on Soto near Brooklyn and he never went to school. His mother Martha would let us stay there and smoke, with music blasting. We never knew if we would make it to school. Vickie and I would party with Danny, Ruben, Tony and Dickie. They were Little Dukes. Josie, Bernie, Patsy, and Chugie would also be there. Danny went for Josie in a big way. Martha allowed them to party in Danny's room by themselves.

It was during this time that Vickie got her first tattoo. Done by Danny. As I said before, if you had nothing to do, you put on a tattoo.

It was about this time that Bernie and I decided that we wanted to stay out all night. Everyone did it, why not us? We told my mom that I was staying at Bernie's and she did the same. Now most girls, in order to take this chance, must have something big to do right? Not us. We just wanted to be able to say we had. Raul Martinez, Tony, Danny, Bernie and I stay out in the cold dark night. I can't remember where we went first but I remember we found an apartment building that had a second story porch with stairs that led up to it on 4th Street and Chicago. We spent the whole night keeping quiet and cold. No one was boyfriend or girlfriend so there was no messing around. When the sun came up we would sneak downstairs and go home. It was only about seven and Mom would ask what I was doing home so early? I know she knew. I slept the day away.

Vickie reminded me the other day about a few instances that happened when she entered Lincoln High School. When I went back to Lincoln High School, Vickie went with me. As she was walking down the hall I guess a few teachers noticed how tight her skirt was and into Mrs. "Chickadees" Honn's office she was called. "Well they may have let you wear your skirts that tight at Hollenbeck, but here we wear them respectfully. You will loosen them." As Vickie says, "It was already loose."

Vickie reminded me that when we went into Lincoln we weren't sure what we were. We sang and lived like Blacks, but we weren't. We knew we weren't White, so what was left? We had no knowledge of who or what we were. Our families had been here for so long they had their own language and culture. We took for granted that everyone ate tortillas and that everyone made tamales. In the Gardens you had all cultures mixed. We ate cornbread and yams and sang Rhythm and Blues better than the Blacks. Lincoln was the rude awakening. We were different. What's this? Mexican? As Vickie said, "What the hell were we?" The Anglos at Lincoln knew what we were and let us know it.

When I transferred back to Roosevelt, Vickie stayed at Lincoln and hung around with some of the girls from Hazard. Dory and Vickie still hang out together and have held each other up in many family crises. Dory lost David Martinez (Weasel) to an early death and Vickie lost her love in a horse riding accident. We stay in touch but I'm here and they're there. How do you like that? Dory got David "Dimples" after being Patsy's and my spy.

CHAPTER TWENTY-SEVEN: THE POLICE WERE ALWAYS AFTER US

One thing at that time, we didn't mess too much with drugs. White port and lemon juice were enough for us. One time we even went with Monko on leave from the Army to Little King's Chair where we blasted joints and drank Green Mint Gin. I feel sick just thinking about it. We got so high I was not in control of myself. We all got messed up. I learned from that because I always wanted to be in control of myself. I got shocks all through my body from pot and I became paranoid. We all did. We just knew the cops were watching us. It wasn't worth it to us. My hangover was so bad I think it lasted two days.

You know how silly the police were at that time? They would send a white, crew cut team into the Gardens to try and bust us. We would be sitting at the flagpole and up would drive this fixed up car and out would jump Pat Boone look-a-likes. "Hey, you got any weed, pot, joints?" "What are you talking about, man?" we would answer. "You know, we need some bad" they would reply. "What is weed?" we would ask. "Well do you know where we can get some?" "Some what?" About then, they knew we were leading them on and they would leave. Talk about a crack up.

One time I remember, Josie, Bernie and I went out with these guys who played in a band. They were potheads and we didn't toke up with them so when they took us home they asked us if we wanted some. With that he opened his sax case and opened the little box in it and it was FULL. He said, "Help yourself" and we did. We made a joint as big as the one Cheech and Chong had in that movie they made. I think he regretted asking us.

The next morning we get up, threw some old clothes on and headed for the Gardens. Where I lived the cops were always patrolling and as I said before they couldn't get into the Gardens. As we are carrying IT, we feel like everyone knows what we have. Over the bridge and we are at the office. Little Mary comes out and we call a few more and then we go on the bridge, commando style, and toke up. Well, Little Mary starts running and we had to chase her and tackle her. Her heart was going so fast and she keeps saying the Devil is after her. There stands Bernie in my old jacket with a pin holding the back up saying, "stop it." Bernie starts walking fast and we follow and when we get to the church she starts crossing herself over and over. I had shocks and just knew the cops were going to get us. We walked down Soto Street like that and after that I stayed away from it. I don't care who takes it; I just got bad reactions.

The police were always after us. I remember coming home from the show and the cops would pull us over to their car just because of the way we were walking. They would make the girls open their jackets to see if you were pregnant. They liked to search us. We didn't know our rights. Actually at that time we had none.

One time when I was going with Sonny, we were headed out somewhere and it was Josie, Freddie, Sonny and I. We went down by the freeway and past the Stillwell Motel. We see cops hiding and then they come out of every place and stop our car. All I know is I had a cop with his gun drawn and pointed at my head yelling "open the door!" I couldn't; I was scared and looking at the end of a barrel of a gun. He kept yelling and I got the door opened. He yanked me out and threw me against the car. I saw a guy we all knew in the shadows talking to the cops. They came over and said we had messed up their stake out. Not an apology just we had messed them up. They told us to get out and we did. I never told my mom about it. Now I want all of you out there to think about our situation. Our parents couldn't do anything. There was no father. No car. My mom was paralyzed. Who could you go to? You know, one of the things the girls talked about all the time was what would a normal family feel like? Like if you were at a dance and needed a ride you could call your mom or dad. None of us even knew what a father's arms felt like. Like if you were with a drunk or punk you could call your parents to come for you. We lived by wits alone. We had no rights so we lived our own rules.

Some of the girls, I will not name them, became potheads and that was their kick. Some went to drink and some went crazy. We had a few who couldn't deal with life, as we knew it. I think with me, I saw too many of the guys that I went to grammar school with be totally destroyed by the time we were fifteen. I do not judge them because I have learned that the higher the I.Q. the more they realize the hopelessness of our lives. They are the ones who really go off the deep end. I learned this by working with this "type" later in life. You see them destroy themselves rather than having society do it. Look around and you will see what I mean.

Soto Street was considered mutual ground as far as the gangs go. Anyone could drive this area and nothing would happen. It was different on Brooklyn. Here was the beginning of Flats. They had different names for different areas but it was all Flats. The Brooklyn show was considered the Brooklyn Flips, which was a part of Flats. I remember one time Monko had gotten a van and all the guys from Hazard had gotten in the back and taken a cruise down to Flats. When they got to the project, Eliso Village, they jumped out the back and jumped some guys. A few nights later Little Mary, Big Mary, Tito and I went to the show and when we came out it was pretty late and as we started to walk a car cruises by slowly and then they recognize us. It's the guys from Flats. We take off running and you had to go down Mott Street to the bridge that crossed over to the

Gardens. They cut us off and we ran to this house that had its lights on. We knocked and a little girl answered. "Help us, there are some guys trying to get us." "Who's there?" her mother asked. "Some Mexican girls. They need help." "Close the door," her mother said. So she did. I wouldn't ask for help again. We hid and they passed us. Then we ran like the wind and made it to the bridge. Once on the bridge we caught our breath and we all looked at each other and knew we had just had a lesson in life. Nobody is going to help you. These were just four teenage girls asking for help. Even if she didn't let us in, she could at least have called the cops or better yet, turned on her porch light. This would scare most people and in those days they didn't shoot you, they just beat you up.

CHAPTER TWENTY-EIGHT: JOSIE'S GREAT HEARTBREAK

Well back to the great move. On the day we were moving to Soto Street, Eddie and Gilbert and Ernie all helped us. Eddie got a truck for us and when we were moving in a group of guys came over and Ernie knew them. They helped us and introduced themselves, Ruben, Tony, Dickie and Danny. Danny Alarcon was nice looking and of course, went after Josie. By now Eddie had learned that Josie was not to be had. He would always walk her, feed her, and even buy her things but she would just mess around with him and never go around with him. He picked up the pieces many times as Josie had one heartbreak after another. She would always get a crush on the guy that was the untouchable. Josie dated Danny Alarcon and when she was fifteen, had a little girl with him. The school was the one who found out she was pregnant and sent her home. I didn't know any of this until she got pregnant the second time (when she was older). Then my mom got drunk and told me. When the school sent Josie home they called the police and it seems Junior heard everything. He never told me. I understand it was a big hearing at Hollenbeck Police Station and Danny was told to stay away from Josie. This was the only reason they didn't arrest him. I was told Josie had T.B. and had to go away to Olive View, a hospital in Angeles Crest. I believed it. Actually she was at a home for unwed mothers run by Saint Ann's in Los Angeles. I know she had a little girl and she named her Catherine. She was adopted and Josie always wanted to find her after she grew up. Mom would go visit Josie with Junior in a taxi and dumb me thought she took a taxi to the mountains. Yep, I only wish she had gotten to see her baby. It was handled wrong. This was 1954. I have to add this. After Josie's death and because I had promised to find Catherine, I DID. Thank God for computers. I will not reveal her name or where she lives but I just wish that Josie had lived to see what a wonderful daughter she had.

CHAPTER TWENTY-NINE: FLUNKING OUT OF SCHOOL

Now at Hollenbeck Jr High after Bernie was removed, the counselor called me in and just stared at me. I don't know what he was staring at. Could it be my shaved eyebrows? My short skirt? My overlip? I know…my hair. After a few seconds he says, "Whom are you trying to hurt?"

"What?" I didn't know what he was talking about.

"I have your Iowa test scores and they don't match your grades. You don't have credits to graduate with and no chance of graduating with your class. Do you know you have zero credits?"

"What's a credit?" I ask. He just looked at me and asked how I had gone on to the eighth grade with no credits. Then he saw my confusion and explained to me that each class had five credits and then he showed me my cumulative card.

"Didn't you ever talk to a counselor?" At Lincoln? Don't be silly, I thought. I felt sick when I understood. You see, at Lincoln High School they just passed you. You got F's and they sent you on to the next person. They only humored you until you finally quit.

You could tell he got it and he left the room. When he returned it was with a different attitude. He was in for the long haul and he assured me that if I tried they would help as much as possible. I was hanging around with Vickie then and we walked, talked, and dressed alike. I have to include this before I forget. Vickie lived on Wabash and she would pick me up in the morning and we would walk to Hollenbeck. Chugie and Patsy would walk with us too. We all wore our jackets. Our arms through each other's, we would march to school cracking our gum. But, you see, with them it was different. They learned. I guess because they had gone from elementary school into a junior high. Not like us - straight into a high school. Teachers taught at Hollenbeck. It was a learning experience for me. We would hang out across from school on Matthews Street and toke up but when that bell rang we would head for class.

Working with the counselor I took B7 Social Studies, A7 Social Studies, and B8 Social Studies along with my other classes. The teachers gave me extra time to catch up. Mrs. Kennedy was the ninth grade advisor and she helped me to reach my goal. In the ninth grade I made up English and I was lucky, I liked P.E., so I was up-to-date in that class. Later, when it came time to graduate, they let me graduate on stage and gave me a blank certificate. I went to summer school at Stevenson Junior High and made up my math. That summer I met my cousin Frances Zamora. She was Tutie's younger sister and was Dolly's age. It didn't matter about the age difference. We clicked and I had a ball at Stevenson. She was going to Roosevelt High after graduation and so were most of my friends. I enjoyed the experience at Stevenson and when summer school ended, I went back to Hollenbeck to get my diploma. I showed up at Mrs. McDonald's office and then she called the principal and my counselor and they all gave me my diploma and they clapped. I will never forget that nor will I ever be able to thank them. My life changed and I now knew I was, if not smart, at least normal. I owe everything to my counselor, Mr. Connors, and he doesn't even know it. He woke me up. Now I could go back to Lincoln. I had behaved myself and could return. All the girls were glad.

Back to Lincoln I go and what happens? The same thing. I go to Ham's and then the rides come and I start to ditch with Bernie and Josie. I just remembered an incident I must tell you about. This happened before we really knew Bernie. At Lincoln one day a newspaper was put on the bulletin board. It was about some students from Lincoln ditching with these guys and wrecking up in Angeles Crest Mountains. The picture was on the front page and all you saw were these two big feet sticking out of a sheet. It was Bernie. I thought she was dead. I had an appointment with the eye doctor about more surgery, and while I was at the General Hospital, I looked for Nordella. She was in the accident too. Bernie was her roommate and she was pretty broken. Her pelvis was broken and she had some stitches. Nordella broke her jaw and it was wired when we saw her. The driver, I think his name was Henry from the Hot Doggers in Rowen, had the top of his head come off and his whole head was stitched.

Now here I am doing everything over again. Why did I work so hard? I walked myself into the office and transferred myself. We now lived on the border of Roosevelt and Lincoln High Schools. I went to Roosevelt and a lot of my friends were they're studying. I still messed up but it was repairable.

CHAPTER THIRTY: BERNIE AND OUR HAIR-RAISING EXPERIENCES

Bernie moved to Baldwin Park and we discovered the El Monte Legion Hall. It was within walking distance from Bernie's. She had lived for a while off 4th Street by Hollenbeck Park and her mother decided that she had to get away from us so off to Baldwin Park. It just increased our field of boys. The Hispanics from Los Angeles went out there for the dances. I know many people who went to the dances that I would have enjoyed meeting then, right Macario. Oh that Johnny Otis had such a show, the "Three Tons of Joy" along with a little girl that sang "Soldier Boy." It was dark and the music was great. Dancing was fantastic. We would get rides back to Bernie's and we would get drunk. We got a ride home one night from someone Josie met. His name was George Rodriguez. I met my next boyfriend, George's brother Richard. When we got to Bernie's house her mom was up and she was mad. Her brother Paul was egging her on and we just waltzed past her and went to Bernie's room. Bernie always said "just keep moving'" and she will give up." Sure. That woman's little feet would walk to the room, throw open the door, yell in Puerto Rican, and then stomp off. A few seconds later here she would come again. This would go on until she got tired or Paul would shut up.

The next morning we were to go to church, her church. They sang a lot and Bernie's mom always made me go. She thought Josie and Bernie were the devils and I could and should be saved. While I was with her, Lydia, and Johnny (Bernie's little sister and brother), Josie and Bernie slept. I was sick with a hangover but I couldn't show it. When we got home from church we were to go to a rodeo Bernie's brother Paul was in. It was a picnic too. Guess who was out rowing with Ms. Podovani and kids? Me. Josie and Bernie were talking to these cute cowboys. I escaped and joined them for the rodeo. We sat on the fence that held the bulls. The cowboys said not to and we asked, "Why?" We found out soon enough.

A bull came bursting through the pen and as Bernie and I jumped, we left Josie up on the fence. She was stuck and had to wait until the bull got its head stuck in a corner of the fence to have these cowboys help her down. Josie's luck. The rest of the rodeo was spent drinking beer and meeting cowboys. When we went home I had a phone call from Richard and he asked me out. He was from Whittier and was nice. He sang with mariachis and his brother was in the same group. He sang songs to me on the phone and so began my love for mariachi music. He sang "Mi Vida." (I now have four mariachi grandchildren.) He was a bodybuilder and was my first mature boyfriend. He almost fainted when I told him I was only fourteen and in junior high. But he came back. We dated for a while and his brother George got to date Josie. Yes, that was how it worked. They would both come down with guitars and sing for us. My mom was so happy and so was I. Richard broke up with me because he said I was too young for him and this was just because he was nineteen. I was heartbroken and mad. No one broke up with me. So back to dating I went. Here I was being faithful and this happens to me. The nerve!

Bernie would come into Los Angeles and then we would get her rides home on Sunday. We would go to all kinds of parties and one time we went to a party in Flats, remember Bernie? Josie, Bernie and I decided to go to the restroom. In I go first and the door shuts. I turn and there are the older girls from Flats. Phina and some others were there. I almost died. I stayed as cool as I could and wondered how Josie and Bernie were planning to get me out. Had they called the other girls? Were they trying to get in? I was lucky and one of the girls that was there, Bibi, said, "That's Blinky, she's okay." They let me go. I could have kissed her but you had to act cool. When I came out it was with all those girls and they were friendly. Where were Josie and Bernie? Holding each other looking guilty.

We had many hair-raising experiences. One time we went to a party in Hoyo Mara and this girl walks up to Little Mary and says she is messing around with her boyfriend. What the heck? We had just got there and we were with Horserace from Hazard. Apparently, the boyfriend used this as an excuse to start a fight with Little Mary. Yea, they came after us. We all jumped in the car and headed for Hazard with two cars after us. Thank God they didn't have guns. We get to the Gardens and head for the flagpole and the guys from Hazard were there. They come out swinging but before anyone could stop the "supposed boyfriend" breaks Little Mary's arm. The guys chased them out but the girls challenged us to a fight the next night in the Project at the office, 8 o'clock. We say "sure anytime." This was done mostly in *pocha* (zoot suit Spanish) and Little Mary is doing fine - along with Big Mary and all of us standing behind her. Josie is next to her. Josie tried to speak Spanish and everyone got quiet. I can't remember what it was but it was not any kind of Spanish. The girls gobbled her up into the group and nudged her to the back. She made us look stupid. Like we weren't using our heads. It was settled.

We all made an agreement to meet at the office on Wednesday night for the fight to determine who won something, I guess. We all meet at the office that Wednesday and make sure we have all we need to meet the enemy. Little Mary, "Sticks?" Yeah. Big Mary, "Chain belts?" Yeah. Blackie (Janet) "Chains?" Yeah. We're set. It turns into evening and as we wait, we get our adrenaline flowing. We're going to knock the shit out of them, we tell each other. The hour is upon us as we wait on the steps of the office so that we can see the hill. Nobody can come over the hill on Lancaster without us knowing. To enter the Gardens you have to enter on Lancaster or

Murchison and if you come over the hill on Alcazar we can still see you before you can see us. Ask the cops. They always tried to sneak into the Gardens. The clock keeps ticking and when it is half past we know they are not coming. We yell "La Hazard Grande!" and we are delirious not because we won but because we didn't want to fight in the first place. I mean I was a freshman at Roosevelt and Little Mary was to be married in a few months to Andy from 38th. But you couldn't let your Barrio down no matter how old you were or where you had gone. Hey, even Bernie was there all the way from Baldwin Park." "Que Pasa?" Josie the Spanish speaker says. "Yo tengo huevos?" "You do?" we say. Everyone laughed. Josie doesn't know why we are laughing. I think that was the last time as teenagers we ever all gathered together at one time.

We are losing a lot of our friends to the service and one of the reasons was that when the guys got in trouble, the judge would say the service or jail. More and more you saw guys in uniform walking through the Gardens and were they cute. I lived half in the Gardens and half out. I would go to school with my homework and after school I would walk home with my friends and then head for the Gardens when the sun went down. The weekends were spent at my house because I lived on a busy street and all the guys would pass and we all would sit on my porch until a car would stop. Sometimes we knew them, sometimes we didn't. We soon would, though, if they had a nice car. They would ask one of us to go for a ride or cruise Whittier. Everyone cruised Whittier and showed off their cars and we all would jump in. Let's go! Josie was never the same after she had her little girl. She would be an obnoxious drunk and I was always saving her butt. All the girls at one time or another had to save her. The guys liked her drunk and she would take off with them. This is what would get her in trouble with their girlfriends and so when she got a boyfriend she would be crazy about, someone would try to mess with him just to pay her back.

CHAPTER THIRTY-ONE: GETTING HIGH

One of the girls that joined our little group was named Angie and she lived in Lincoln Heights across the tracks. She and her mom lived alone in a four—apartment house. She brought a girl named PeeWee in and that brought the girls from 38th into our group. Now we traveled back and forth between East Los Angeles and the westside. We would hang out on Alameda and Florence and it was a sea of new guys. The girls from 38th had more access to cars and I remember PeeWee getting a yellow Ford she could hardly drive… our first car. We would all go to the parties and the beach in this car, get drunk, and then ride around and put our money together to get gas. I'm talking pennies. Nadine and Maggie also were with us and Maggie lived in a warehouse that had one-room apartments. She was the nicest and most common sense one. Through Maggie we found out that a factory near her house on Mateo Street under the 7th Street Bridge would hire you without proof of age. You had to be sixteen to work then. I was just 15. We all got jobs that summer. It paid 90 cents an hour and this is how we got our money for gas and beer. I had to give my mom half of my check of $33.33 and put some aside for school clothes. We would get our checks on Friday and PeeWee would pick us up and we would go to Dearden's on 7th and Main Street and cash our checks because they didn't require I.D. Bernie would come into town or we would go out there and we would party until the wee hours of the night. Many a night Bernie, Josie and I would try to sneak in and Mom would be waiting in a chair for us. She would sit in a chair smoking a cigarette. She would wait until we got in and then scare the hell out of us with "Okay, what time is this for you three to be getting in?" After 2 a.m., only the drunks are out on the streets. We would keep from laughing until we got in our room and then we would become hysterical. We would talk in the dark about the guys we had met or the party we had been at. One time we got home late and as we opened the door Mom was not waiting for us. She had fallen asleep. We closed the door ever so softly and looked toward our room. The house was dark and we could see the outside light from the lamppost shining through our bedroom window. We tiptoed to the doorway covering our mouths so we didn't laugh and BANG we hit the door. Lights on. Mom had shut our door and the light was the reflection from the front door. Bad time. She yelled and we said "Yea Mama, tomorrow."

In the morning she would give us the silent treatment. That's okay because my head would hurt so badly. We would send the twins (Ronald and Donald) to the store on the corner to get us some Pepsi or Coke and chorizo. After we ate we would wash our hair and set it in pin curls for the night's events. Friends would come over to see what we were doing that night. Our house became the headquarters for everyone.

One Saturday morning we were sitting around talking at the kitchen table and Bernie said, "Have you heard about Coke (soda) and aspirin?"

"What about it?"

"If you mix aspirin with Coke you can get high." Off we sent the twins (we always had to pay them to go) and back they come with the bag. "Here, they didn't have any Coke so we got you Pepsi." No aspirin so we got you Alka-Seltzer. Into the bedroom we go. After locking the door we decided this might work. We push the Alka-

Seltzer into the pop bottle and a big explosion sounded. Soda gushed everywhere. Mom's yelling, "What are you doing in there, let me in!" The only thing we could do was have Bernie stick her finger in the top to stop it. Mom comes in and we try to look innocent. She knows something is up but she is not sure what. She closes the door and goop falls from the ceiling. You should have seen the looks on our faces. Bernie's finger was stuck in the bottle. We had to work all day to get it out. To this day Bernie and I start to laugh every time we think of it.

Josie was at Roosevelt High now and she hated school. Little Mary was engaged and Andy was in the service. Bernie was still in Baldwin Park and Big Mary was working with Little Mary. Big Eddie was at Roosevelt High and would give Josie rides to and from school. One time, Josie, Bernie, Babe and I went to a dance at Evergreen Park, and when Josie and Babe went to the restroom, they took too long and I went to see what was up. When I walked through the door this girl named Sandy had Josie by the hair and was trying to hit her. Sandy must have weighed 200 pounds and was huge. Babe was washing her hands looking scared. Sandy kept saying, "I hate you." She was an Anglo who thought she was Mexican. I was scared. I jumped on her back and started to hit her and it was like hitting a balloon. She didn't feel it. All of a sudden she looks at me and flicks me off her back like a fly. She had loosened her hold on Josie long enough for her to get out and I was on the floor. She followed the fast walking Josie who tried to walk with dignity, head high with a roll of toilet paper dangling from her hand. When Bernie sees her she takes her out the side door and we all meet up. Sandy is still mad somewhere in the dance and we take off. Wrong barrio, wrong girl. As we go down Fourth Street we can almost hear her footsteps coming after us. I am the first to admit she scared me. She was too big and she didn't feel pain. I asked Josie why she wanted her? "I don't know," she said. I think we all slept with one eye opened that night.

The next day everyone comes to tell Vicky and me that Sandy is talking to Josie outside the school on Matthews Street. Vicky and I run and Sandy is talking to her real nice. Thank God because I just couldn't go through that again. We get Josie and start to walk home and Eddie drives up. We get in and he asks her what happened. She told us Sandy had said she was high on weed and that she knew her boyfriend from Garretty liked Josie and she was sorry she had done what she did. "It's okay, I know how it is," Josie tells her. We all look at each other and laugh. We later found out that Eddie had told Sandy to apologize or he would beat her up. He told her it was the same difference as her beating on Josie. Eddie loved Josie so much; she, of course, liked him as a friend. To me Eddie was a big brother. Many a time he would walk into a party and if I were high he would pick me up and take me home. I would sing

"Good Night Ladies". He would just mumble at me. Eddie was from Lopez Mara. He was popular at school and a good student. Eddie went into the service right after graduation and soon Josie gained weight. Guess what? She was pregnant. This time Mom was mad and told me about the first one. She told Josie that this time she would see it through. It was okay because this is what Josie wanted. At that time. Later when it kept her from parties and in the house, she would be mad. In those days you didn't get pregnant without getting married. If you did, you were a *puta*. Who is the father? She wouldn't say.

Gilbert, Ernie, and Eddie walk Josie and me to Angie's house on Eastlake in Lincoln Heights and there is this guy sitting there staring at me. He is getting on my nerves. He gets up and asks me to dance. No one is dancing. He is high and in his case I do mean high. He will not leave me alone. He asked me to show him where the bathroom was because it's in the back of the house. I go to show him and he starts kissing me and I push him away and go back into the front and told Josie "let's go." We took off with the guys and never wanted to see that guy again. Angie called the next day and says, "Why did you run from Sonny?"

"Who is Sonny?"

"He is a friend of mine and he never goes for anyone like he went for you."

"Sure, I could tell by the way he attacked me." She tells me he is a good guy and he wants another chance. No way.

"He wants to take all of us to the Diana Ballroom, come on," she says.

"Well where is he from?" I ask.

"The Avenues." Yea the guys from there are cool. I was fifteen going on sixteen when I started going out with him. He was twenty-one. He didn't look it and I looked older. We started dating and we broke up a thousand times and went back together. On my sixteenth birthday I was with him and when the girls sang "Happy Birthday" I had them include "sixteen" in their song. I think he almost fainted. He stayed away for a while but not for long. He bought a '56 black, hardtop Chevy. He lowered it and had gold fiesta hubcaps with gold lights under the fenders. He put two spotlights that we would use at the drive-in. We three sensible, sophisticated young ladies undertook many adventures.

CHAPTER THIRTY-TWO: TOO GOOD TO PART AT DEATH

One time I remember, Bernie and Josie were talking to the cutest guys at Roosevelt, led by Earl Chavez, and it was summer. The guys made a joke and Josie, being Scarlet, laughed so ladylike that holding back caused a bubble to escape her nose. She had a cold. Now according to Earl, the bubble came out and dangled there, long as a foot, and Josie takes a deep intake and it all goes back in her nose. Every time Josie would walk down the hall Earl would make the gesture of a bubble dangling out his nose and being sucked back in. Ahhh, yes, we were sophisticated.

Once we walked into a dance at the CYO in East Los Angeles and they started playing the record called "The Letter." Bernie had gone around with a guy named Tommy from Rowen, and that was their song. They had broken up a few years before and every time it was played, Bernie would dash somewhere, usually across a room, crying and we all would follow her with words like "don't worry" or "he's not worth it." Well this time she dashed for the window and flings her head out but the window was not open. CRASH!! Everyone looks at us and Bernie just wants to get out of there.

The girls dated the guys from the Calliveras, skeleton heads, and Josie dated Kiki and Bernie dated Florico or something like that. They were "fine" but they had no cars. The guys that had the cars were 6'6" and weighed 100 pounds or 5'2" and weighed 200 pounds. Guess which one's I went out with? So parties would find me locked in a bathroom or out in the yard keeping one step ahead of them. They always got fresh and so I would stay out of their sight until the ride home.

Earl Chavez was the singer, joker, and all around man of many talents. Josie and Bernie were constantly at each other's throats over Earl. He would be with one on one week and the other the following. They both thought that he was theirs. The funny part is that they both knew the other was dating him. I think it was always like that. If Josie wanted someone, then Bernie wanted him. If Bernie wanted someone, then Josie wanted him. So began a love/hate relationship that lasted years.

I remember one time when we were all at Hollenback Park on 4th Street and the fog was just coming in. We all had stopped there and Earl started walking on the bridge over the lake with his hat on and his raincoat over his shoulders. He lit up a cigarette and very dramatically sang "Man in A Raincoat." Wow, he almost had me going. I can still see him.

We all met him on time, at his request, at Wabash Playground and he was singing with a band then. The name of the band was Cesar's. We backed him up on a few songs and then sang some. It was good rhythm and blues but they didn't want that, they wanted "Red Sails in the Sunset" kind of music. It was their loss. We had enough adventures to last four lifetimes, Josie, Bernie and me. I feel there is more to come, even after death. We were too good to have to part with such a thing as death. We had a good time in spite of our circumstances and held tight to our dignity and looked for the adventure over the hill. Thank God we had each other.

I remember one time Josie had gotten a job at the May Company downtown because she had been out of school because of her pregnancy. You couldn't see it yet and she needed the money. We all needed the money. Well, Bernie and I think it is a beautiful day and why should we all be locked up for the day? Josie leaves the house like she is going to work, I leave like I am going to school, and we wait for Bernie on Brooklyn and Soto. Off we go because it is a beautiful day. What do we do? Head to the show downtown to see *The Girl Can't Help It*. As we settle in the dark theater, Bernie gets out the Viceroys. In those days you could smoke in the balcony. We light up and this fire comes from Bernie's cigarette. She lit the filter and it wouldn't go out. We almost had a fire but the funny part is she didn't notice right away and was sitting there with this fire on the end of her cigarette.

Bernie and I decide that we wanted a good job like Josie's so we dress up and go to the phone company to apply. Now you must understand we were only fourteen or fifteen. I wore a red velvet dress with a black velvet boat neck collar and rhinestone earrings that dangle. I wore nylons with a rhinestone butterflies at the bottom of the seam. Hair pushed to one side, I thought I looked mature. Bernie was dressed the same but had on a full lace dress with net in the front and on the arms. Of course a lot of makeup and we were off. The personnel woman kept a straight face the whole time she interviewed us. I think we made her day. I must say she was very nice and didn't laugh at us once. So much for that. As I said before, the only job that we all could get was at the egg factory. I worked there three years in a row to get money for school clothes. I would work all summer and then I would get to keep a whole check for clothes. Mom seemed to think food was more important. One thing I did buy was a lock for my bedroom door. I caught my S.O.B. dad trying to molest me as I slept one night. I let out a scream and turned on the lights and he kept saying he was lost. I told my Mom to get him out and this did no good. I put a bolt on my door. I can still picture him standing there in his shorts trying to hush me. Bastard!

The girls would walk up to my house from the Gardens and then we would catch the Soto bus on Sheridan and ride it to Olympic. Then we caught the downtown bus to Mateo. We would walk under the bridge and get our aprons on and crack eggs. Yes, we stood on a plank of wood next to a conveyer belt breaking eggs for eight hours and no talking to the person next to you. Our job started at 7:30 a.m. everyday and it's a good thing we were young so we could take it. On Friday, Sonny and his friends, Fuji and Johnny, would come for us and we would go cash our checks at Dearden's and buy beer and go up to Pot Hill and drink. Fuji was nuts and one day he had too much to drink and when we got in the car he said "tales of the century" and down the side of the hill we go. This hill was in Lincoln Heights and it was steep. Everyone was screaming and as we go down I thought, this is it. I don't know how we did it but he landed in the driveway of a house at the bottom of the hill and we took off. Nothing happened to the car.

CHAPTER THIRTY-THREE: SONNY - WHAT MORE COULD I WANT?

How can I explain the consideration I got from Sonny? He was strong and intelligent. He had a job and he had graduated from Lincoln High School. I mean what more could I want?

Josie's pregnancy was hard on all of us. She would be a spoiled brat when Bernie or I would go out. Remember the bassinet Mom had given to my dad for his baby with the other woman? Now my Mom cried on his shoulder and he brought the bassinet back and we decorated it for Josie. My Mom and Dad now worked as a drunken pair to support Josie...sick. All the girls were a part of this baby. No one had had a baby yet in our group. I never told the other girls about the other baby Josie had. Bernie and I just kept it a secret and now Sonny became one of our group. Poor Sonny would come to take me out and all the girls would jump into his car. We fixed his friends up with them. When Josie had the baby, I called Sonny to take us to the hospital but he was out. We took her in a cab. When Sonny got to the hospital he pretended he was the father. This saved face for both my mom and Josie. My father, not knowing this, lands at the hospital and tells Sonny he is Josie's husband. Boy, did we have some explaining to do. When the baby was born, out of gratitude, we named the baby Rudy (Sonny's real name). When he came home from the hospital I let Sonny go by himself to pick up Josie and Rudy. Later we found out that although she didn't love him, Big Eddie was Rudy's father. 12/21/57.

About March the following year Sonny was picked up for possession and he was sentenced to one year at Chino Prison. In a way it was good because I had time to graduate from high school. I'm sure if he had been around then, we would have married sooner. His car was taken and he served his time. I would go out to see him every weekend with his mother. Chino was far in those days and no houses were out there. Sometimes I did go out with the girls and I was in Little Mary's wedding.

The dance was at the Case Hotel and it had all the girls from Hazard and all the guys from 38th. What a wedding! My cousin David got out of jail and he went with us. This is where he meets Bernie. We all got drunk…let me explain. The night before the wedding all the wedding party had to go to confession and in those days you didn't eat after midnight until you received communion. Well the mass was at ten or twelve and after we honked all over the Gardens and across town to 38th we go to take pictures in downtown Los Angeles. By the time the photos were taken it was late afternoon and off we go to the reception. When we get there they have us serve the guests and they keep giving us beer. No food and they rush us off to the dance. I took some chicken and mole in the car and ate a little on the ride over to the dance in downtown Los Angeles and my cousin stays with us all the time. He gets a twinkle in his eyes and he is about 23 years old and buys us a bottle. Josie, Bernie and I finished it before we got to the dance. We do the grand march and my cousin buys us Tom Collins'. I don't remember the rest of the dance. It turns out that one of Sonny's friends saw I was passing out and told Josie we had better go. They say the elevator door closed and I was standing. When the doors opened he was carrying me. I had passed out. When he gets to the street, some guys in a car say they know me and will take me home. He almost put me in the car but Josie got there and told him I didn't know them and he grabbed me away. To this day I don't know who it was. Thank God "Screwno" was there. They took me home and my Mom said I was just a bundle of lace on the bed. If I remember right, that was the night that Bernie stayed out with my cousin and her mom came to my house and took Bernie back to Baldwin Park after she and my mom had a few words. Of course our dogs decided to mate in the middle of the argument. Bernie is crying, my mom and Mrs. Podovani are exchanging words, and I have a headache.

CHAPTER THIRTY-FOUR: BERNIE AND JOSIE GET MARRIED

Bernie left and she and my cousin start dating. Soon they get married and have the wedding at my Aunt Aurora's house, my cousin's mother and my father's sister. We wore the same dresses that we wore for Mary's wedding. Josie was dating Ben Torres going out I put cold cream on my face and set my hair Saturday night so I couldn't go out even if I wanted to. The night Bernie got married I remember the Angeles Crest Mountains were on fire and it lit up the sky. Bernie and David were married in front of the fireplace and my Uncle and Aunt looked happy. I think they thought Bernie would tame him. Not that boy or was it the other way around.

Well, Josie stays out all night with Ben and when she comes home, after drinking all night good old Mom and Dad confront her and Ben and ask them what they intended to do about the situation. Ben blows their minds by saying "we want to get married." Josie borrows my chemise dress and they go to a chapel and get married. Josie was so happy and of course I was just glad that she was married. Josie always slept around looking for love and now she had it. Baby Rudy stayed with me. I would come home from 38th and I hardly knew him. I would come home from school and he would be on the porch to greet me. He kept me busy and people saw him with me and assumed he was mine.

On Sundays I would go with the girls to Elysian Park. Everyone went there and I would go with Sherry, Margie, Chocolate, Nadine and all the girls from the Westside. They would be on the hills and would drink and talk. All Sonny's friends were there and they were now dating these girls. All my friends were married and even in school everyone was gone. In our group everyone had quit school. When our group was first there we hung around with the girls from White Fence. Even my cousin Frances was gone now and the only one left was Carmen Estrada. We couldn't stand each other. One day I asked her "Are you going to finish school?"

"Yes," she said.

"Let's hang around."

"Okay," she said, and that was the beginning of one of the closest friendships I have known. We did it and boy was I proud. Junior was graduating top ten at Lincoln High. I don't know where I was in my class but I know it was high. Since Sonny was gone I gave all my energy to school. I was in the Glee Club, G.A.A., and Student Service. I worked the attendance office; Mr. Schaffer was in charge and I still remember the day I reported to him. He looked at me and said, "They must be joking." I had had a few run-ins with him. Well I didn't say I was perfect. There were still temptations. Once in a while I would ditch just to stay in shape. I must say we became very close and I got one of the few A's given by him.

Sonny got out just before my prom. He gave me my engagement ring and when I took him to my prom all the teachers ran to meet him. He said he felt like he was stealing Little Iodine. He w**as.**

CHAPTER THIRTY-FIVE
UNBELIEVABLE

After I started dating Sonny I witnessed one of the biggest scares of my life. A girl named Tina had a party at her house on Marengo Street and I was to meet Sonny there. The party was good and I went out to see if he was there yet. It was a house behind another house (a back house) and as I came out I remember "Dopey" from Hazard was standing talking to someone. I was standing next to the front house and it had an alcove space. I had just passed him and I hear this guy tell him "I'm looking for someone." "Who," asks Dopey. "You." The guy puts a knife into Dopey's back, Dopey goes down and Little Stevie yells from the front yard and I see a flash. He had pulled a zip gun and was shooting randomly at all of us. Thank God I fit in the space of the alcove. I was thin and just made it. I watched as shots were fired and lights went off. I saw the guys from Little Eastside fall, reflected in the lights of the bullets, and one guy yelled for his Mama. I just stood there and someone grabbed my arm and pulled me into the house. When the shooting stopped, I got a ride home with someone. I can't remember who. I know it wasn't Sonny. Later I found out that he and his friends were on the bus and were about to get out when they saw the shootings and just stayed on the bus.

The following Monday the school had an assembly and I sat with my friends, Sukie, Peggy and Jeanette (Blackie). I had already gone through being called names because everyone thought it was chicken what Little Stevie had done. They blamed everyone from Hazard. No one could control him. He drove a little green car and we had gone out with him and Little Arnold a few times but that was as far as it went. When the lights went down in the auditorium I felt something hard on my shoulder. It was Baca from Garretys, foot in a cast. "Look what your Vatos did." I tried to ignore him but he just kept on. He kept pushing at my head. I knew better than to say anything. He wasn't even a student there and he was with his friends. I turned and told him "I never told the guys what to do and even a friend of mine was shot, Angel from Little Eastside." Hell, I didn't even know what happened except I almost got shot. I left after the assembly was over - very slowly. You walked slow like you would away from a snake. He just wanted me to show any fear.

At lunch this big mouth girl came over to me followed by a group of friends and starts yelling about my Vatos. Again saying it was "my" Vatos; I didn't have anything to do with it. Anyway, once more the girl was huge. Why couldn't the small ones try to pick on me? I was just getting ready to fight and Blackie, who was bigger than me and mean looking, gets in front of me and tells the girl that we don't own the Vatos from Hazard. You want something from us? Wow!! The girl turned tail and ran. Loved it. The only other time I had been close to someone shot was when Charlie, also from Little Eastside, had been shot right in front of me. I was going out with Carlos from Little Eastside and we went to a party. Charlie was a clown and when he said he was shot we thought he was kidding. He had grabbed his stomach and fallen to the floor. "Get up" we laughed. Then I saw a little hole in his stomach. The guy that owned the house had shot him. He was drunk and standing at his front door with a rifle. I screamed and his wife pushed the guy back into his house. Everyone picked up Charlie and he just kept asking why? We were close to the General Hospital so it would be faster to drive him there, then to wait for an ambulance. Charlie was so scared and we kept telling him not to worry. There were three cars and we all raced to the hospital. We got him into the emergency room and stayed with him until they said he would be okay. We went to see him before they wheeled him upstairs and we told him not to worry. We'll take care of everything. By that we meant tell his mom and take care of him.

When I get home I tell my Mom everything and what do you think she reads in the papers the next day. GANGLAND SHOOTING. According to the newspaper a gang took a gang member to the hospital and told him "not to worry they would take care of everything." Now the police were worried that there would be retaliation for the shooting. It was nothing like that but who would believe us? Oh well, it only made us bad. You couldn't win.

CHAPTER THIRTY-SIX: A LITTLE PROBLEM WITH SONNY

Mom and Shorty, I never called him dad, were doing the lovey dovey thing again with the whiskey bottles and vodka. They would drink to forget and then forget what they were drinking for. At this time it was every man for himself. The twins were turning into punks and I didn't blame them. Bud was bad and Fud just followed. Linda was just a shadow to me. I do remember her hanging out the bathroom window smoking and Junior turning the hose on her yelling, "FIRE, FIRE!" Linda kept saying, "please." "FIRE."

When I was going with Sonny we ran into a little problem. The guys from Hazard were looking him over and not liking what they saw. Here he was coming into the Gardens and taking one of the girls. One night I was sitting at the office with some of the girls and up walks Joe (Clown) and the guys. Well Joe had been in the service and I hadn't seen him in a while. I don't know what he thought he was doing, but he sits down and asks me whose sweater I am wearing. It was my senior sweater from Roosevelt. When I told him this he said "no way." I told him I was graduating summer 1959 and he couldn't believe it.

He asked me if I would like to go to a wedding that weekend and I asked, "who's?" "Mine," he replies. I think he thought he would hurt me this way. I told him I would ask my boyfriend. Just then Sonny pulls up in his '56 Chevy and I said, "There he is, I'll check with him." I left an open-mouthed Joe.

A few nights later Sonny and I are in front of my house on Soto Street sitting in his car steaming up his windows when a car comes real slow past the car and someone yells something. You could hear scraping and when they passed we could see a can opener, called a church key, held out to scrape the side of the car. Jackasses. Well I guess we were lucky, a car can be repaired. How can I explain Joe's wedding? I knew I had to go, otherwise they would say I was jealous. While I was there Joe takes me over to see his mother Vera and it was embarrassing for all of us. His wife Gerry was nice. After a respectable time, I took Sonny out on the porch and told him about Joe and we left.

CHAPTER THIRTY-SEVEN: GRADUATION/MARRIAGE

I had so many things happening to me in 1959 that I just remember it as a blur. My senior year at Roosevelt was the best year of my life. I had many friends both black and Chicano. One person I met was Willie Davis. He was dating my friend Bernice Jackson and his mother had a beauty shop on First Street. He was the best at any sport he tried and in 1958 he won the All City Award. We gave him an assembly held at the football field. He was so bashful. When Bernice introduced me he just mumbled. That's why, later in life when I became a Dodger fan, I didn't believe it was he. He did good. The black girls from Alliso were close to me. I guess growing up in the Gardens had made me color blind. I hope I always stay that way. Jo Edna Johnson came up to me one day in school and told me her boyfriend knew me. Who? Eddie Joe Brown. I just hope he didn't tell her what a monster I had been. When I saw him he was a young man and I couldn't picture him jumping fences like in the old days.

I now was a model student except for a cigarette in the bathroom at lunchtime. Everyone would meet there for the second half of lunch. We were all seniors and one day the principal busted us but she just told us to put out our cigarettes and "leave and not return" or she would suspend us. So close to graduation and something stupid happens. We left but not before noticing that the Japanese girls who were always there were absent. They worked in the principal's office and knew about the raid. Smart. I never smoked in that bathroom again. Well, almost never.

I remember the excitement as graduation drew near. Junior was getting prepared at Lincoln and we just couldn't believe we had made it. Junior and I were close once more and I taught him how to dance. It happened a few years before when he had an R.O.T.C. Ball and no one to go with and no car to take anyone in. Well he had a deal for me. If he could get Bernice and I to go with Gilbert and him, Gilbert would get a car. Sure we say. Now you must understand Bernie and I are beauties and we don't just go out with anyone. This would be a feather in my brother's hat. The night of the Ball, Bernie and I get ready and I have made plans for my then boyfriend Richard to pick me up after the Ball is over. We get to the Ball and all of the little boy's mouths pop open. Gilbert and Junior are the perfect hosts. Then we are dancing and Bernie and I are at least a foot taller than them and Bernie says "I'm going to take off my shoes, okay?" Junior says, "If you do I'll walk off this floor." I was the one dancing with Junior and I tell him "don't you dare." Bernie takes her shoes off and Junior leaves me in the middle of the dance floor. I could have killed him.

Now we were graduating and a new closeness happens. I don't think either of us thought I would do it. I was the only one of the girls to make it. That in itself says something. I'm also the only one to leave Lincoln. All the girls in later life made it in whatever field they chose and this was in spite of Lincoln. Anyway here I was. Junior and I took many pictures in front of our house with our gowns on and life was good. Of course I had to wear my Aunt's shoes and they were a size too small. I didn't care. Sonny was at the ceremony. We were getting married the following Friday. We were married at my church in the Gardens. It was a catastrophe.

First Sonny's church, Sacred Heart, wouldn't give permission and when we told Father Ditman he told us not to worry, just show up. He took care of it. Two nights before we were to marry, we met with Father Ditman and he had known me since my Confirmation at age 12. He had seen me grow up and I know he liked me because I took him seriously. He asked me, "Nellie do you know what you are doing?" "Yes," I answer with stars in my eyes. Nothing went right on my wedding day. First, our best man Danny thought the wedding was at night and was out getting a haircut and washing his car while we were all waiting at the church. The night before my wedding, my father was drinking and acting like an ass. I had asked my grandpa to walk me down the aisle and he was mad. Like he was a father. All night I heard him yelling. Carmen and Ruthie, my bridesmaids had slept over. They were used to drunks.

In the morning I got dressed and my grandpa come for me in his Volkswagen. I had a big hoop dress and it was too late to do anything about it. Into the car I go with the hoop up in the back. My poor twins had to walk. My Mom had made me make Josie my matron of honor. Here she was, nine months pregnant with Benny Jr. She had taken Rudy to live with them and he was at the church crying. In those days, if you received communion you had to go to confession first. This we had all done the night before. It should have been okay, right? Here is the setting: Clouds with sprinkles, church ready. They started the march three times. No, no. Our best man's not there yet. A cab drives up and out steps a drunken man, my father. He walks up to us and tells my grandpa he was going to walk me down the aisle. Grandpa takes him aside. Comes back and asks me "Do you want him to walk you?" "No Grandpa," I say. He goes back to my father and tells him to go sit down. He does.

To get me calm Grandpa tells me "Look, this is the way to walk down the aisle" and he starts bopping. He did this all the way into the church and as soon as we hit the aisle he started to strut. As I walked down, I started crying and this started Rudy crying. As the ceremony began, I kept crying and Sonny gave me his handkerchief and I used it during the service. Rudy is screaming now and it came time to take communion. The best man was not there, and Junior stood in even though he had not gone to confession. So what does he do? He takes the host. I couldn't believe my eyes. The twins were in the front row and they were proud. When Father Ditman pronounced us man and wife, we just looked at him. He stood there smiling and then he motioned for us to kiss. That done, we looked at him again and he said, "That's all I can do for you, the rest is up to you." When we left the church the twins flooded us with rice. I think our best man got there then and was apologizing. The sun came out. At the house after we had taken the pictures, my mom had a party. Grandpa was so cute when we took the pictures. He was the perfect grandpa. He noticed Sonny had no hankie so he put his in his pocket. On our wedding pictures has Sonny with a big W on his Hankie. He looked behind the Curtains of the background to make sure it was OK. The photographer told him to get away from the curtains and this caused a sneer from Grandpa. Back to the house and a drunken party. Sonny went to a bar with my father and I hid in the closet. I'm not going home with him. Josie finds me and gives me a pep talk and so I pick myself up, dust myself off, and start all over again. Josie is the one with the facts of life talk, the wife duties talk, and the start of a family talk.

Grandpa left early and I know he knew what a big difference he made. I think that is what started my friendship with him. I hope when I get to that age, I can be as alert as he was.

Grandpa was a comedy. He and Myrtle went to Yosemite Park and just like a move they decide to take some pictures on a mountain. Well of course, Myrtle keeps telling him to back up. Well, over he goes and is hanging on a root cussing at her. They call the Forrest ranger and he gets him up. Myrtle said she thought he would kill her.

They went to Europe and made the tour. Grandpa said the French didn't know how to build toilets and that he made a mess. He also told me if I was to go to Europe to go while I was young because if you can't walk you miss everything. I am glad I took his advice.

CHAPTER THIRTY-EIGHT: BABIES, BABIES, BABIES

I began my marriage with high hopes and dreams. At first it was all that I had hoped for. I was Donna Reed and Mrs. Cleaver all rolled up into one. We moved into a small house on Romulo Street behind Nightingale Junior High School in Highland Park. We lived right around the corner from a bus stop and Gateway Store was within walking distance. Sonny was on parole and he had lost the car but we would overcome that. He behaved and got his old job back at Nolle Auto Company on Figueroa Street. The bus took him right to it and I would pack him his lunch. Poor guy. I was use to my brothers and their lunches and I would pack 2 sandwiches and a fruit. He would only eat one sandwiched and tell me to just pack one. Next I could only cook for 7 so I had so much waste and would try to save some for my brothers. They would stop down my house and eat. They were from Clover then and were spinning downward. Perfect, now to start a family. It took me almost a year to get pregnant and everyone was looking at me with that look…what's wrong with her? In those days you got married and nine months later had a baby. I went to the doctor and he told me to just relax. Sure…the pressure was on. Josie had Benny and we hung out with them. Babies, babies, babies, that is all they could talk about.

Her friends were not normal. Ben was like a beatnik and played the bongos. I remember one night Josie and Ben wanted us to come over and see their new couch. They lived in Monterey Park and when we got there they had their furniture piled on top of their old set. Pillows on the floor. Ben turns off all the lights and puts on "Quiet Village" and bird noises fill the room. He has the music full blast. Ben had a Ford that he drove like an idiot and we had to get our ride home from him. He was higher than a kite and we almost had an accident. Josie would laugh off his driving but it wasn't funny. The four of us hung out but Sonny was always grumpy when it came to Ben. This was strange because they had so much in common. In the sixties they were always flying high. We got into Jazz and as I was playing house, Sonny and Ben are going after work everyday to see something new. Topless. I hated him when I found out. I would cry, scream, beg, everything, and nothing worked. I finally found myself pregnant and I was so overjoyed I cried. I was so sick. As the time drew near for the birth I was so happy. My Father in Law bought everything for the baby and he just kept smilling. This was his and Angie's first grandchild. We found another house on Avenue 28 and Pasadena and my wonderful Suzette was born. It was a long labor and she was sideways. They tried to knock me out but I wanted to see my baby born. If ever you question God you should see a birth. Only a God could create such a miracle. I couldn't believe I had a baby. She was beautiful.

I must tell this part. For weeks at the White Memorial Hospital, they had tours of the maternity floor and they showed us this red button outside these double doors that led to the labor rooms. I had nightmares about that stupid red button and would wake sweating. When I went to push that button I was thinking, what did I do? This is going to hurt. I knew that there was only one way out and I felt like a trapped animal. We didn't have epidurals, we had what they called a saddle-block and that is like a spinal. They give it to you when you are 8 or 9 centimeters...why give it to you? As I enter the labor room I hear this woman screaming and I break out in a cold sweat. "Am I going to get that bad?" I ask the nurse.

"Honey, you're just beginning." Oh my God, what have I gotten myself into? I had my Suzette and that woman was still screaming. I was further along in my labor than her. Afterwards I kept telling nurses "I did it, I had a baby." I was twenty when my first was born. It was the first of four. Two years later came my nut Annette who was followed sixteen months later by Rudy Jr. During this time my husband would go to work with a big breakfast and come home for lunch. After work he would drink with his friends and come home just in time for the kids to be asleep. You want to talk resentment. I remember many times I would sit with his meal while he was with his friends. Sound familiar? He was good as far as not going out socially with his friends but now I was still young and very pretty. I had not gained any weight and motherhood suited me. We started going out every Saturday with his friends and this is when I met my *comadre* Rachel. She and Alex (Moe) would become our best friends. We had our babies together and she had boys, I had girls. When I had Rudy I talked her into trying again. I told her, "Look I had a boy and percentage wise, you have to have a girl." Oops! I was wrong, another boy. Our kids were raised like brothers and sisters and we stayed close.

When we had Suzette's baptismal party it was held in the Avenue's with all the guys from Hazard there. Yep, we had Monko and Big Mary baptize our first and so this brought both gangs together. We had many parties and gatherings with, of course, Joe and Jerry along with their little boys. Monko (Richard Garcia) and Mary had a little boy and a girl named Cindy. That party was the biggest and best party I have ever been to. All the guys were perfect gentlemen and I was so excited because that night Josie had her only girl, Lorraine. The ceremony was at the Plaza L.A. as was the family custom. Firstborn had to be baptized at the Placita because of the family. This is so they could keep track of all of us. I don't know why. Freddie and Richard along with Joe were at our house a lot. Sonny went to the store with them, too. I don't know why but it always took them forever.

When we started to hang around with Sonny's friends it was okay because I had known Alex Rodriguez from Lincoln High. He hung around with my three stooges, Ponchi (Rudy Corrales), Wahoo, and Poncho. They used to delight in making my life miserable. They were juniors at Lincoln when I was in 8th grade. While I was walking with my friends down the hallway they would throw blackboard erasers from the second floor and hide, just to see me looking for the culprit. They also had thrown me into the pool at Lincoln Park with my clothes on. After that they would call me *mujara* (wetback). That day at the pool I had been standing at the door watching everyone having fun. I couldn't go in because I had no eyebrows. I, being the smart person I am, had shaved them because everyone had high eyebrows. I wanted to go in so bad. Anyway, all of a sudden I just felt hands pulling me. Have you ever gone completely blank because something is happening to you that is so bad you can't believe it? Well that's how I felt and the next thing I knew I'm in the water and people are laughing and pointing at me. I could have died but instead I walked out of the pool with my head held high and no eyebrows. That was the last summer I shaved my eyebrows.

Rudy is the only one alive of the three and he is still my friend. It is so nice to have someone around that can remember the spring of your life. I just get him quiet about our friends when he tells us of all the deaths of our friends. He was and is a friend of my husband's and comes to Tucson once a year with his wife Mary for the Mariachi Conference. He still hangs out with our friends in Los Angeles and brings us all the news on what's happening. I never thought we would grow old together.

CHAPTER THIRTY-NINE: THE SIXTIES

We all went through the sixties with all its drugs and parties and although most of us came out okay we lost some on the way. My *comadre* Rachel and I made a new group with Margie (who was married to Richie Gallegos) and Helen (who was married to Ralph "Baby" Paez). We all became *comadres* and *compadres* and we all got our hair done in high curls and took diet pills to stay slim, that is, all of us except Rachel. She could eat the refrigerator and not gain an ounce but if we so much as looked in the fridge we gained. Short dresses and husbands that left us with the kids while they went to the store. God we were stupid. We would all go out to the Club Huntington in El Sereno and everyone would be there. Afterwards everyone would go to our house to party and we saw the sun come up before it ended. This was an exciting time. We would dance the latest steps like the "twist" and "mashed potatoes" and our skin was still young. We were the ideal pair. Sonny couldn't dance but I always had my brother Bud with me. He turned out bad. I mean he was handsome and his eyes were so beautiful that every girl tried for him and I had to keep him from fighting. He had a hot temper and if anyone looked at him he would challenge them. Drugs had a lot to do with it. He had the name Lion and he only had one son. Ronald Jr got in touch with me a few years ago and we both were so excited.

He came to visit me in Tucson along with his wife Tina and their 2 little girls Julie and Sarena. They had a boy last year and named him Ronald. I know Bud is smilling down or up at them. Only kidding down.

I want them to know how much my brother loved Hobbie as he is know to us. Hobbie is much more serious then Bud was and is putting his family above his friends. He is just as cute as my Bud and I hope to keep him in my life.

CHAPTER FORTY: COMING OF AGE POLITICALLY

Notes and pictures reminded me of one of the saddest memories I have and that is when my friend and protector, Big Eddie, died. This guy was one of the nicest people put on this earth. He didn't do drugs, at least not the needle. He would drink and blow pot but that was it. I was expecting my first baby any day and when I went to my mother's house on Avenue 30; she looked awful. Everyone is tiptoeing and I knew someone had died. They wouldn't tell me who. Josie and Ben went to the wake and I kept asking who died? The next day Josie tells me it was Big Eddie. It seems that they found him dead in a garage and they said he had had an overdose. No way, I couldn't believe it. Not Big Eddie. I would go for years to his grave and leave him flowers or introduce my children to my friend. It later came out that a weasel named Wetback had given him a bad dose and left him there to die. He could have been saved. I never saw Wetback again but I sure was looking. He married my friend Patsy when she was only fourteen and pregnant. Her family gave her everything and they had a good home. Wetback somehow convinced Patsy they were keeping a great love apart so she ran away with him until she was pregnant. Her mom was almost crazy with worry. The last time I saw her, she had six kids and looked like hell.

Her sister Chugie was bad but she turned out right. Became a nurse and she with skirts so tight they sent her home from school one day! She was given a bad deal with her parents. Who can explain?

While we were off in the great American dream, Junior was in the Air Force. That was the only thing open to him in those days. We had no money and no one told us of the Pell Grant or any grants. As I said before, Lincoln really let this boy genius down. He had all the potential of becoming anything he wanted, but no money, no education. He was given a scholarship for one hundred dollars. Boy, you could sure go far on that. I think this was the best break he ever had.

The Air Force recognized his potential and sent him to Yale. There, along with other classes, he studied Chinese and soon was on reconnaissance flights over China. My little Junior was fast becoming a man. While he was in training, he had his first experience with prejudice. He was in a restaurant in Texas with some friends who were Chicanos with dark coloring. The waitress told them that they didn't serve Mexicans and they would have to leave. When my brother got up to leave, they said "Not you, just them."

"I am one of them," he says. When Junior went to the service he was the apple of my mother's eyes and when she bid him farewell, it was to a short, crew cut boy with eyeglasses. After the service, my brother went to Berkeley on the G.I. Bill and then we got word he was coming home. Everyone was there to meet him. Mom was living next door to me on Avenue 29 at the time. By then, I was truly Donna Reed. Up pulls the taxi and out steps this tall, longhaired, sandal-wearing hype. Mom cried. Junior was to open our eyes to the movement, over my God Bless America. I accused him of being a communist. I wouldn't listen. I would not believe that there was anything wrong with our government. When I saw the picture on the cover of *Life* magazine I sat down and cried. How could we? The children looked like my children and one picture showed them crying and the next they lay dying with our bullets. I then started looking at the statistics on how many Chicanos had died in this rich man's war. The people in Vietnam didn't know the difference between communist/democratic government. I started thinking…danger.

The topper was a trip my husband and I made up to Stockton to visit some friends. We all decide to go to Lake Tahoe and I was excited. I had never been to a gambling place and I wanted to go. I was expecting my son then. You couldn't tell. Up over the mountains we go and when we get there, it is late. Snow covered the ground. Ray and June (our friends from Stockton) are both nervous when we pull up to a motel. "What's wrong?" we ask.

"What if they don't rent to Mexicans?" they say.

"What the hell are you talking about?" I answer. We go in and no questions asked. I couldn't get over it. I was raised in Los Angeles. I learned this made a difference. After our weekend there we head back to Stockton and Ray and June take us to a nightclub. The singer is white and she keeps making demeaning remarks to the band, which was Mexican, and calling them the Frito Banditos along with other things. I couldn't stand it and when she said to them that they had better behave and remember the Alamo, I yelled "and who won it!" Well, my husband almost died and the other couple turned red. She came to our table afterward and apologized. I made her sweat. POWER! When we left Ray and June, I think they breathed a sigh of relief.

On our way home I encountered my first full-blown act of prejudice. To this day I still can't believe it. We were coming down Interstate 5 and we were hungry. Being from southern California, I was not accustomed to the ways of the north. We pull off to eat at a cafe in this little town called Greenfield. We walk in and it becomes quiet. When we sat at the counter I noticed an old wrinkled white woman staring at me in the mirror. I made a face and you would have thought she had a heart attack. The people were all staring and the waitress ignored us. I got it and hoped my husband didn't because he would have been hurt. I was mad. I would not leave until they served us. She finally did and this was only because she knew we were not going to move until she did. I couldn't eat but I sat there. When we left my husband left his food too, put two cents as a tip. We left laughing and when we looked back at the window they were all staring at us with their faces at the window. We stared back. When we got in the car we took a spin around the town and what we saw made everything clear.

On one side of the town, the houses were big and white with yards. There was a big church. This was where the growers lived and on the other side in shacks lived the workers. No big houses, no church. Children playing in mud. I hated that town and when we left I think my fate was sealed. Too bad none of the people who were so against the movement had been exposed to that little town. Maybe they would understand what the fight was about and what Cesar Chavez did. He made a miracle happen.

I had been so smug and thought I was right in my Donna Reed role. When IT hits you, you don't understand how IT was under your nose so long and you didn't see it. IT is large and ugly and you know IT was slime all over your past and you couldn't wash off. For shame the way people justified it.

I took my glasses off and saw it. Ugh.

CHAPTER FORTY-ONE: HOW TO RAISE KIDS

I more or less lost track of Terry and Bernie during this time, and only because we were sisters did Josie and I talk every day and take our kids to the park. But we had a difference of opinion on child raising. I still believe in discipline and she believes that children should express themselves and act out their feelings. Nope. Only in a positive way, I felt, and every time we had our kids together they would fight and would destroy my kid's toys. I also spank. I did not beat but if the child was bad, she should be punished. I will match my results with anyone. We're talking respect. Josie's kids had none. They used and abused her, led by her husband Ben. I'll just say she tried to be Betty Crocker and they rejected her. She kept trying to the end. Rudy is the only one who showed her love and tried to make her happy. Little Benny did make a giant turn after he married Linda and became Jehovah. During this time, Ben is dealing and gets Josie involved. He gets her hooked on "Reds" and "Bennies." I hated him. Josie didn't make much sense during that time. She was always high because she thought this was the way to hold onto Ben. Poor fool. He was having an affair with some broad who lived across the street from his silk screening job. My brother Bud told me and he didn't know what to do. I told him just leave it alone because Josie would not believe it. Sound familiar? Here we go with the rose-colored glasses again. Who said history doesn't repeat itself? You could watch Josie going crazy and her kids right along with her. The only difference was that Ben gave Josie and the kids a lot of money. I mean hundreds and they couldn't buy love.

I myself got hooked on diet pills. Doctors were giving them out like candy. I liked them. That's why I stay away from them now. When we built a house on Avenue 29 (I designed it), we had another surprise. I had been trying to have another baby and I finally did it. Of course the doctors wanted me to stay slim so they kept giving me my diet pills. I delivered Christy Ann two months premature and breech. She only weighed 4 pounds and I had her natural and tried to help her as much as possible to survive. I kept blaming myself. They kept her in an incubator and I went home empty-handed. You can't describe the empty feelings of leaving a child behind. I lost so much weight and my nerves were on edge. When she came home I turned into a nut. I sprayed everything and everyone with Lysol. I also made masks for people to wear around her. At the hospital, White Memorial, they would have me scrub just like a doctor and wear a mask. They would then take my baby out of the incubator and hand her to me to nurse. I did this in front of a big window in the baby nursery and everyone could see me. I didn't care as long as she made it. She did and has been a pain in the butt ever since. If it were to go wrong, it would be with Christy. We called her Christy Catastrophe. I blamed myself but it turned out I had a tumor in my uterus and it pushed her out. At the ripe old age of 29, I had a hysterectomy. I was just glad I had the four children, Christy included. I couldn't take losing one anyway, and I had come close.

Now I became super mom, no more fooling around. Our house was done and Rachel and Moe baptized our Christy. I would walk my kids to school each day, I didn't know how to drive, and tutor some of the students. I liked this and soon I was working for the Los Angeles Board of Education. I had kids coming every forty-five minutes. I would rush home at noon to make lunch for Sonny and back to school I walked to pick up the kids. Now instead of diet pills, I was able to buy Bennies 10/$1. A lot cheaper and Sonny could always get them. I stayed slim which at the time to me was so important.

I will never forget my students because they broke my heart. I couldn't just lock the classroom door and leave the problems behind. One student was Johnny; he stank so badly none of the teachers wanted to teach him. After talking to him I found out his mother was a waitress and had boyfriends. She didn't get up in the morning so he would eat lunchmeat and give some to his baby sister and walk to school. One day he came to my room with his hair slicked down with cream. His face was clean. He would help me with my work. He was turning around. One morning, he came to my class with burn marks around his neck. I asked him what happened and he tells me this mother's boyfriend had hung him in the dining room. He trusted me. I went to the office and reported it, like you are supposed to, and they called the police. The police got to his house and no one was there. The next day he didn't show up for class and I thought the police had saved him. No, when they had gone back to the house, the family had moved. To this day I don't know what happened to him. He trusted me. I hope he made it.

Another boy, Salude, was a depressed boy. His teacher, Mrs. Jones, had brought me a picture he drew of a boy hanging. She asked if I would work with him. I did and you know what his problem was? He was poor and very smart. When I paid for his pictures at school, he brought one to my house. He thanked me and he progressed very fast. You must help quietly. He learned phonics and was off like a bullet. The name of the school was Hillside Elementary and my husband had attended the same school. I worked hand in hand with many of the teachers and when the famous teachers' strike in Los Angeles 68 came. I was right out there with the teachers. I also got parents to walk the lines and carry signs. Everyone thought they were supporting the teachers in a good cause and many of the parents had never experienced a strike. I told them about the way the school board passed our school by when it came to new buildings (we had bungalows) and new books. The teachers were good but their hands were tied. Most of the teachers bought their oun supplies and stayed after school tutoring. Mrs. Jones had the children first and she was bilingual. This helped her with her students and gave me my first look at the concept of bilingual education. I saw it in action and know it worked. I saw kids who were labeled all of a sudden understanding what was going on and learning. The word bilingual has been given a bad name because it was misused.

Bilingual ment learning a lesson in English and then in Spanish, Vietnamese, ect. Not just taught in their home language with no reinforcement of English.

CHAPTER FORTY-TWO: OUR TIME - THE CHICANO MOVEMENT

Now begins the story of my involvement in the Chicano Movement. As the book begins... it was the best of times, it was the worst of times, but it was our time... a time to stand up and say "What's wrong with this picture?"

After the strike was over the teachers went back but I couldn't bring myself to. When we were striking, the teachers gave credence to what many of us already knew. It showed us how the system had failed us and now they wanted us to go back. No! There were too many Johnny's and Salude's. Then I got a phone call about a group of women who wanted to form an organization. They had been on the strike lines and felt the same as me. The meeting was at Laguna Park on Whittier Blvd. I said I would go. I didn't know what to do or how to dress so I went as Donna Reed. I mean I had on a dress, heels and nylons. I listened to this short, beautiful lady tell us, or rather explain to us, what we had been feeling all our lives. For me, it had never been put into words before and when the next meeting was held, I went in a skirt and flats. By the third or fourth meeting, I was in a sweatshirt, jeans, and sandals. Later came the headbands and boots.

The first step of my independence was <u>my car</u>. I bought it with the money I made working for the board. My husband kept stalling about teaching me to drive. "The street's so small and the car is so big" or "if you hit something you will wipe out the kids." This used to work but I had to get to my meetings and I kept playing with the gears in our driveway and soon I turned the key and went bouncing down the street. I went to Hillside to get my kids and Suzette was crying to the teacher "Don't let her take us. She can't drive." Silly child, I explained, as I bounced down the street. Gears were hard. I can still picture this man driving a Frito truck. He had a red light on Avenue 35 and Pasadena Avenue. I came down Avenue 35 and bounced across the intersection and he just laughed and put his head down. I just waved as I rode my car past him. Soon I was a pro and this released me to do what I know I was meant for. I joined with my brother, Junior, on his ideas of the government. Brown Power was now a sound that was growing loud and more people were listening to Rose Lopez and Rosalio Munoz. Even old folks were coming out and soon all of East Los Angeles was a movement.

There was a Chicano Moratorium held at what was then called Laguna Park to protest the high number of Chicanos serving in Vietnam and to protest extreme police brutality in the area. Young men like Tony Valdez and Little Johnny were found hung. We were told they hung themselves. Sure. So, on this day everyone came out with picnics, blankets, and families to join in the Moratorium. Most of the youth was marching down Whittier and Some on Brooklyn. We were at the park waiting for them. Police had surrounded the park, waiting for something to happen. One guy went across the street to buy a six-pack of beer and on his way back, got shoved by a policeman. He shoved back and that was all it took. The police moved in beating and clubbing everyone. They even ran into a bar on Whittier where an LA Times reporter, Ruben Salazar, had ducked for cover. They opened the door and shot Salazar dead. Eventually Laguna Park was renamed Salazar Park. So when the police had their riot at Salazar Park, it confirmed what everyone knew. Salazar had been writing about the police brutality.

It was now or never. Never have you seen so many united Chicanos. I am just glad that I was there at that time in history. I met some of the most dedicated mothers and educators and hope they continued on with the struggle. We wanted to stop the poor treatment of Chicano kids and also to try and change the future for them. We wanted EDUCATION for our kids. Is that too much to ask?

This is a hard story to tell because it seems like a million years ago and a different world. It was a time of closeness and sisterhood of Chicanas. We had united in a common cause, our children. We had waited for the men to get our children's rights and then we found we were more effective in fighting the systems. More important, we had Rose Lopez. Rose was four feet of energy and smarts. She was the motivator. She was the mountain shaker. She was the founder of Parents Involved In Community Action (P.I.C.A.), a parent group from East Los Angeles and in 1968 I was a member. Rose called us P.I.C.A. because we were like chickens with an issue. PICA, PICA, PICA until we got our way.

I, along with Mary, Gloria Barkoff, Rudy and Monica Salinez (he was from Macy), and Josie, were her board. There were others but we signed the papers when we became incorporated. Oh yes, Rita Figueroa. How could I forget her, she lost two sons in shootings on Arizona Street in East Los Angeles. She was a fine lady and she fought harder after her sons' deaths.

I'm sorry I can't remember everyone's name but we were too numerous and only a few stand out in my mind. I remember Olga Castaneda because she started a chapter in San Diego when I started one in La Puente (which will come later).

P.I.C.A. met every Wednesday evening at Laguna Park and we were mean mothers with no shame at all. The fact that we would demonstrate at the drop of a hat proved this point. That is what scared the "biggies." They knew we would strike and it could get ugly. We struck at their homes, offices, and even their lunch places. We would show up with parents at schools when they didn't know their rights and help them. At first the principals said we couldn't do this, but we proved them wrong legally. They freaked out when we asked for the child's "cume card[6]." We had workshops to learn what to look for and what to ask. Damn we were good. We became famous for our attacks. We even went in our curlers and no make up with kids in their pajamas. We had a phone tree and if you got the call you went. None of the excuses used now. I think that, above all, made us successful. We were mean but we had every right to be and the more we learned about Title I programs and monies that were supposed to be for our children, the meaner we got. We got things done and many of us took that first step into Chicanoism.

Many marriages were over and many women experienced violence for the first time in their marriages. All this because we refused to stay home and we stopped waiting for permission and just did what we knew had to be done. Our husbands felt threatened and many times our meetings would be interrupted with a loud bang from a door being swung open and there would be a husband red in the face and breathing fire. He would yell at his wife, "Get your fucking ass home or I'll kick it all the way home." We all went through this. Mine would always be drunk. I myself remember when we had the Garfield walkouts and my husband had left for work with a warning not to go. No I'm staying home. He left and so did I. Down we went and the news was covering it. This always happened and of course, our friends the F.B.I. were taking our pictures. They thought they were hidden. We're carrying the signs and the press is taking pictures of my daughter Christy doing the arm raised "Chicano Power" and then I realize what time it is. Home I rush with a tail on me and as I turn down our street, I see Sonny's car in the driveway. Oh God! He heard about the demonstration on the radio and knew I was there. We had a real fight then. Now we had begun to get physical.

I waited until the following week. I knew he was drinking and I couldn't go on like this. I saw my kids suffering because of the fighting and because he was always mad. I put the kids in the car

---

[6]   Short for cumulative school record.

along with our dog, Scooter, and clothes. I locked up my dream house (which we had lived in for about 4 years) for the last time and we left. I remember being so scared and knowing I had these four little ones depending on me. I turned the key. Off I went to a house my sister Linda owned. She lives in Alaska and was glad I was moving in. No lights and dirty but I felt safe. This was in Rosemead and Sonny didn't know about it. I felt sorry for my Mom because I knew Sonny would be down there looking for me. She loved Sonny so much I knew she would be hurt.

Only if you go through something like a separation can you truly understand how many lives it affects, not just yours. Sonny was roaming the streets looking for me and kept telling people he had changed. I believed him because I wanted to and he said he would go to a counselor. He never did. I told him we could not live in Lincoln Heights and so we moved to La Puente. I had been active for four years and was trying to salvage a mess of a family. Sonny said he would stop drinking. Sure. I said I would stay out of the movement. Sure.

Like everyone who had that taste of the movement, you could not sit back and not do something when you saw injustice. It's in the blood. I started a chapter of P.I.C.A. and soon after, Fred Aguilar approached me. He had a wild idea that we would have someone from our group run for the school board and that person would run under La Raza Unida. I told him "this person" did not stand a chance and he said, "Sure you do." Me, no way! He brought in his reinforcements and they talked me into it. I was the first Chicana to run for office in Southern California, as far as I know in all California. I have found out from a wonderful Chicana Studies Professor, Raquel Rubio Goldsmith, that there were three Chicanas who ran that year. One in Texas and one in Colorado and of course, me. What an honor! I wish I knew their names but, of course, just the men are remembered. I read Guzman's' United We Win, and although I was interviewed I receive a small mention. This was still their world. If I had known this was such an important part of our history, I would have kept notes. Maybe I'll ask the F.B.I. for their pictures and notes.

This was early 1973 and La Raza Unida was in its glory. It had grown and was now considered a threat. We would still meet with the organizers in East Los Angeles in a top floor office. Yes we had an office. The posters of La Raza Familia would decorate the walls. I explained to them and the corps from La Puente that I had no knowledge of politics; my knowledge was in education and if something went wrong and I got elected, I would be in trouble. I remember the head guy's name was Gilbert and he had green eyes, and you know I'm a sucker for green eyes. "Don't worry, this is just a scare tactic and we know you won't win. Trust me." Boy I always fall for that line.

Then it started. Fred and Larry Duarte took over and they knew what they were doing. Kind and gentle Eddie, Larry's brother, entered the picture now. He set up the time and places where I was to speak. Eddie gave me the speeches and sent me out in front of man-eating Anglos. They wanted my blood and I was sure they would get it. How dare I, a simple minded Mexican WOMAN, run for the Board under La Raza Unida! I was not a good speaker and I knew it. I was trying too hard and I was so young. I wish it were now. Boy would I give them a run for their money. You have to understand, I had gone from Donna Reed to La Chicana and now they wanted me to become a smooth-talking politician.

The Raza in La Puente worked so hard it was unbelievable. I was amazed. My biggest support came from Tali and Che Garcia. They worked the people who were walking and they, no, Tali, got things done. He and my husband would go out in the night and signs would be all over La Puente and Hacienda Heights by morning.

CHAPTER FORTY-THREE: HEROIN AND BUD - A DIGRESSION

My brother Fud was attending Mount San Antonio College in Walnut, California and made me go, too. He pulled me over to the College and after I went, I found I loved school. He wanted me to just go to school and get a degree but I studied Chicano Politics and some history. United States, I think. Everything was so interesting and I was just trying to capture knowledge. So now I was a student, mother, candidate, and activist. Fud, now know as Donald, was married and had served in the Navyand seen a lot of action. I took him a few times down to P.I.C.A. and he knew what I had to do with my life. He had had the same experiences that I had as far as being labeled early in life as slow to learn. E.M.R.[7] for all you educators. We were both smart, just raised as stupid. You know what gets me is the fact that I learned to read even though I see double. I think I am a miracle. I did better because I was street smart but he did better because of the Navy. I think if he hadn't gone into the Navy he would have died on the streets. Just like Bud.

---

[7] Educable mentally retarded

Bud and Fud were from Clover and they had fights and GTA[8] along with a near fatal fight that had them arrested for murder. It wasn't them and they were let out after they were cleared, but it was with the understanding that Donald continued school and after graduation, enlist. He did and a smart Donald appeared. Bud, on the other hand, stayed on the street and used to carry his pill bag with him and it had everything you might want. Bennies, Reds, you name it, he had it. He would fight at the flick of a hat and if you looked wrong at him, he would kick your butt. My Bud. He had girls who would do anything for him. He married his high school sweetheart, Carmen Luna, at a very young age and they divorced. She went on with her life and I know she would later have a baby boy by a man known as "Tin Man." Donald had four kids and they are doing well. He owns a home in La Verne and a cabin in Big Bear.

Who would have thought that twins could be so different? My brother Bud died of an overdose on May 5, 1981. What a way to remember Cinco De May. He was found in a rundown hotel across form the general hospital. He had been hooked for a few years and we all tried to take care of him but it was no use. I lived in Tucson when I found out he was hooked on heroin. I was in Los Angeles for New Year's and when my brother Bud got to Josie's house, my mom told me. She was dying of cancer and wanted me to take Bud home with me. He got there with Mary and I got a stick from a tree and beat him. Here he was a BAD BOY and I was beating the hell out of him. I remember he said, "Nellie, I can beat it."

"No you can't, no one does. You know this Bud, why? Why?"

"You don't know how it feels; it makes you float. There is no feeling like it, I can handle it, don't worry," he said.

Sonny and my kids arrived in Los Angeles and I remember they were teenagers and they loved their Uncle Bud. He had lived next

---

[8] Grand Theft Auto

door to us with my mother for a few years and my children became very attached to him. He would baby-sit for me and actually <u>play</u> with the kids; I think he was trying to capture the childhood he never had. He would play practical jokes on them and they loved it. He would sing and play guitar to my daughters and they loved it. He would take them one at a time to the racetrack and let them choose horses and they loved it. He would call them Mija and Mijo and they loved it. My kids knew they had a special place in his heart, in his life. He was the Uncle everyone wanted, fun, fun, fun. He had all their love and he was the one who would break their hearts. I told my kids to watch their Uncle Bud die. No one beats the needle. This was a lesson for them. They were teenagers and I could not of taught them this from a book. Thanks Bud.

He stole everything to support his habit. Fud took him in and he stole his car. Josie took him in and he broke her window and took off with her stuff. He even went to Alaska with Linda and left with dirty hands. The last time I talked to him he had called me and he was making no sense. He said he had a dream that he had died and he was making his own coffin. He had the nameplate and everything. I told him to please stop and he said he couldn't give up his fix. He had just taken one and then he started saying "Buddy, Buddy, Buddy," and he hung up. The time I saw him was at his funeral. Poor baby. My handsome baby brother was found on the floor of the third floor hallway of a fleabag hotel across the street from the General Hospital. No one knew who did it. Certainly, not the cop that found him. He had said he would get my brother but he didn't know who did. My brother's face was so smashed in that I didn't recognize him. I thought they had made a mistake. Then I saw the nose and I knew it was him. We had to have a veil over the coffin opening it was so bad. His wake was on Brooklyn and Floral and I remember it was a rush job. Even the priest was in a hurry. The Dodger game was on and as we were in the visitation room, we could hear the game being played loud. Poor Bud, not even his funeral was held with dignity..

That was the last time I saw his son. He was there and he looked like Bud. The priest just said a short "see ya" at the cemetery and he was gone. I have his cross next to my Mom's. When my mother died on November 9, 1980, six months prior to Bud, it was an end to an era and her funeral was held with all the dignities she deserved. My grandpa had given my Mom the grave next to her mother, Josephina Violet Zepeda Reyes. This was in prestigious Glendale's Forrest Lawn. See I'm jumping the gun again. Let's get back to the movement…I told you never a dull moment.

CHAPTER FORTY-FOUR: VIVA LA RAZA

I can't remember all the names of the people involved but I remember the hard work they did. It was a trip seeing all our people working together for a common goal. I just wish I had been more prepared, I didn't know what to do. I dressed wrong. I spoke too soft and I couldn't keep the sarcasm out of my mouth. It was hard. I couldn't play the game. The people had fundraisers and bands played for free. Food appeared out of nowhere and people were just so enthusiastic that it rubbed off. It was like a dream and I did try hard because of these people and their faith. They were poor and yet they gave what they could. I will always remember how excited they were and how they would shake my hand like I was someone they could trust. That's what the word trust was. I am still amazed at how many older people were registered La Raza Unida. If you saw them you would think they were conservative all the way. That's what I meant about the dream of La Raza Unida. It was a good concept and it made sense. We have never been represented in government and we did have the numbers that called for a say in how we were living and how we should be represented. I still believe that and now that we have some representation, we must remind them of this.

The MECHA students at Cal State ran an article about me and of the coming election. They said they were proud that I, as a Chicana, was undertaking this election challenge. WOW!!

I had people calling me from all over California and this made it even harder because I could not win. Didn't they know that it was a scare tactic? As the time grew closer for the election I was attacked openly at meetings by the candidates and was set up many times by their supporters. I was accused of being a racist. Me? I think the truth hurt them so much they felt obligated to attack. We had no one from La Puente on the school board who represented La Puente and Hacienda Heights and only one Hispanic. Sure I was a racist. Who wouldn't be? They told us who our principals would be and here we were the majority minority and no Hispanics in those high positions. Sound familiar? They told us how our kids would be educated and if they were to be educated. They had great shop classes. They attacked because they were scared. On the night of the election, I was at home with my family and a few close friends when the doorbell rang and there were people from Cal State with a movie camera and reporters. The air was full of excitement. We had wine and food brought in by neighbors and friends. The house was full. So much hope. We kept calling for the scores and I got a funny feeling when they said I was in the lead. God help me.

Everyone was talking loud and taking pictures and they all were saying, "when you win" and this went down like a ton of bricks. I must have turned white, no pun intended. When my friend Jan Miller (she was also running) came to congratulate me, I knew I was in trouble. She said she had just come from election central and I was third. This election had three seats up for grabs and it looked like I was doing it. Then in walks Fred and when he came in his face was down to the ground. He said, "we lost." Just like that. We all looked at each other and you could feel the sadness. Everyone had tried so hard. We all made small talk for a while and tried to pretend that our hearts were not broken. Soon everyone left. What an empty feeling. I had gotten caught up in this election and was surprised to find I really wanted to win. I came in fourth and that was much better than we had anticipated. This did not help. We felt a great letdown and I got drunk. I slept late the next morning and it was like someone died. You know, no one knows what to say. We all got together and tried to find out what went right and what went wrong. We tried to act professional but unless you go through it you won't understand. It hurts. I guess it was the idea I got that I was the great brown hope. We still worked on projects together but it was never the same. Our hearts were not in it. "Next time," we all said.

CHAPTER FORTY-FIVE : MOVING TO TUCSON BY WAY OF EL PASO

We closed the office and continued with our work but we had lost the feeling of closeness that a campaign gives. Fred was our link to what was happening in the party. About this time, I can't remember if it was June or July, my husband got an offer to move to Tucson. We had wanted to move some place where our kids, by this time entering their teens, could grow without the fear of gangs. He made the trip to Tucson to check it out and he took our eldest daughter Suzette with him. I am sure she hated it. When he came back he said it was great and that we should move. I had mixed emotions because I come from a big family and I would have to leave them all behind and go off to the wild lands of Tucson. Were there cowboys and Indians?

As we are making plans for Tucson, Fred tells me of a big convention being planned by La Raza Unida in Texas. He said we should all go to represent La Puente. We had a meeting and at this time we were told we would all leave on Thursday and meet in El Paso. Well we couldn't leave until Friday and we were told that everyone would have stickers of La Familia for their cars and we would receive help or whatever on the road if they saw the sticker.

The sticker would tell other convention travelers we were all together in this great odyssey. I was sort of nervous about leaving by ourselves, but what the heck. I packed the kids and off we all went. We traveled all night and when we came to this turn off in the middle of the desert we decided to sleep a few hours. We got off at a street called Park. It was in a little city called Tucson. This was really out in the boondocks. We slept and then took a highway called Benson Highway to hook up with the freeway to El Paso. Hummm, I'll have to think about that move to Tucson. I didn't see anything there. It was HOT!!

When we got to El Paso, the convention was already under way and we met up with the rest of our group. I remember the sun streaking through the windows at the top of the auditorium. You could feel the electricity in the air. I was feeling like a child going to a fair for the first time. People all over the place and everyone talking. When we got there all hell was breaking loose. There is a big split in the way everyone is feeling and in who should be the leader. I remember being asked to go to a meeting in a small room and seeing the leader of the East L.A. chapter. He was speaking to our group, along with others, about a vote and he was for supporting Corky. We were asked to support him. I did not know what it was all about but you got the feeling something big was just about to happen. When we went back to our seats I was shocked to see Mexicans or Chicanos from places like Illinois, Minnesota, and many more states that I always thought were populated by all Anglos. You must remember I never traveled east and had just taken for granted that the east was White. It was an overwhelming feeling. I was so proud to think of all these people, my people, under one roof. Then I heard the yelling and madness coming from the center platform. It was our great leaders. I felt sick. We were doing it to ourselves again. I think everyone thought the same thing. It was like our dreams exploding in our faces. Why? I think they should have had more woman on the power side and let us all in on what was happening, not just the selected few. The egos of the men got in the way of what was good for the common folk.

As I said before, politics were not my bag. Education was. But were they both the same?

There was so much confusion and noise; you knew it was the end. The end of all our work, the end of people's dreams. Political power for our long deprived Raza. I still feel sad when I think about what we could have accomplished. I think we still do it to ourselves. There are always those EGO'S to contend with. Five steps forward, two back. Oh well, a step at a time.

I was so upset that I did not notice that my little girl, Christy, age three, had wandered off. Each thought the other had her. Everyone started looking for her and they made an announcement but people were leaving and most did not even hear. I was so scared and frantic as I searched each and every crack and cranny. I was hysterical and I yelled and still no Christy. (A friend reminded me when I told him of this event, of La Llorona, looking for her children, screaming for them as she searched). The thought of what had happened to the one man on his way to the convention kept popping into my mind. All he had wanted was water and he was killed. Could people hate us so much as to take my child? We were going to go to the police and we ran for our truck across a big parking lot. There were still many cars and I don't know what we thought we would do. Stop all the cars from leaving? I was crazy. There she was. She was sitting on the steps of our truck waiting for us. I didn't know whether to spank her or kiss her. I told you, Christy Catastrophe. Thank God that she was safe. I must tell you that during the convention it had been announced that one of our delegates from Colorado was shot asking for help at a gas station. This was in Oro Grande and it just showed the hate that was felt toward our people for trying to organize. What if someone had taken my little girl? It was a different time and we were speaking out for the first time and everyone felt threatened. We all felt fear. Fear of the ride home and what could be waiting out there. We decided to visit some relatives in El Paso and get our heads together. You should have seen their faces when we drove up. Me with my headband, poncho and bell bottom jeans and my husband with his long hair. My husband's cousin "Tuty" and his wife Nena probably thought we had flipped. We tried to explain about La Raza Unida and they humored us. They made us feel at home and to this day they introduce us as their activist relatives from Los Angeles. It was a different time. You either had it or you didn't. I must mention one very strange thing that happened to me. My father-in-law came to visit me, right in the middle of my involvement, and he cried and kissed my hand. I asked him what was wrong and he told me a story about when he had first come to the United States.

Rudy M. Bustillos was from a proud family in Chihuahua, Chihuahua, and when he was a young man he decided to come to the United States to make his fortune. Back in Chihuahua his father was a judge and my father in law was the youngest of eight children. He told me he had been very spoiled and was not weaned from the breast until he was three or four. He would play in the yard and then he would find his mom and nurse for a while and then play again. When he crossed over into Texas, this was back in the 1920's, he was walking on the sidewalk and some white men came up to him, pushed him into the street and spit on him. "Mex walk in the street," they said. He died of shame that day. He never forgot and he wanted to thank me.

Well back to the story. When we got back to La Puente we started to pack. We said our good-byes and I felt sad at leaving everyone. My mom and Josie were crying uncontrollably. We stopped to say good-bye to Tali. He was confined to bed with back surgery and he meant so much to me. We had gotten close with the campaign and he had worked extra hard. He really believed in me. I felt like I was leaving a part of me when we loaded the trucks. My brothers Arnold and Donald drove one of the moving trucks to Tucson. They did not believe we would go. Even when they left us in Tucson, Donald said he looked in the rear view mirror and saw me. He wanted to go back and get me. When we left Los Angeles, we passed my campaign signs still on the poles and I wept.

Here I was in that little city we had passed so long ago on a dark night on our way to El Paso. It just seemed so wrong. Many nights my husband would get home and I was packed to go back to Los Angeles. Thank God we stayed. My kids grew up gang free and got a halfway decent education. I grew to love Tucson. Now I would not leave.

I swore I would not get involved in anything in Tucson and would just be a housewife. Once more good intentions. I worked the first few years and we had to get on our feet. The move cost us a lot. People who were renting it ruined our house in La Puente. They never paid rent and we had our rent here in Tucson so we were trying to pay both a house payment and rent. My husband's job was not working out and many times it was my pay that saved us. Yep, resentment. Both of us felt it. I was working my home life away and we were living in an apartment that only had two bedrooms. No yard. No street, just dirt on St. Mary's Road and Cuesta Avenue. Mud when it rained and no grass. My car got stuck in the mud and I had to get a push out. My kids were raising themselves and I felt like I was in hell. My kids got lice at Manzo and their hair had been long. I had to cut it. I had no phone. I called my mom from a booth and said I want to come home. "Come back," she would say and I would pack my bag again. One day my eldest, Suzette, said that while I was at work my husband had taken them for a ride. They had passed a house for rent and they were not supposed to tell me about it. "Where is it?" "Down Silverbell." I found it. Three bedrooms, two bathrooms. It had been neglected and it was rundown but it was a house. I called the owners and rented it.

The house had no grass. It was a mustard color and inside some of the walls were painted a dark maroon. Doors were cracked and no screens. We rented it and moved in against my husband's wishes. He was happy where we were. He had it made. He was hanging out with some guys and I guess it was mid-life crisis for him. I started drinking and gained weight. What a joke. I would bring home my six-pack from work and wait for him to decide to come home. My poor kids. I quit work. Now the ball was in his park and he had to take over. I wanted to save the mess again. Many times we talked divorce but we just lived in a quiet hate. I started working with my kids and then we tried to sell the house in La Puente to buy this house. NEVER RENT A HOUSE OUT IF YOU ARE NOT NEAR TO HANDLE IT. The law protects the renter. They lived there for free and when they left in the middle of the night they broke all the windows and just destroyed the house. It was a four bedroom, two baths, built in patio with pool and they destroyed it. When we had bought it we put down five thousand dollars. We got one thousand for the house after commissions. I thought my husband would have a heart attack. We used the thousand for our down payment and you know what? We fixed the house and it is the most love house in Jollyville.

CHAPTER FORTY-SIX: TITLE I AND TUSD

I went back to work and that is where I met a lot of the community and my friends. Irene Echevarria was a young lady that turned into an activist during our friendship. I was her supervisor at T.G. & Y. and talked to her along with other young people about what to do about the injustice here in Tucson. Education wise that is. Sound familiar? I worked until I saw that my daughter Christy was not getting educated and was getting D's on her report card from Tully Elementary. Why? Well they explained to me that she was getting help from Title One and she was just a little slow. Great shades of brown. They are acting like I am an idiot and don't understand Title One. They had no idea I had been on the State Advisory Board on Title One in California and use to train people on Title One. I quit work and started to work with my daughter to improve her grades and guess what? She went from a D to and A student in one quarter. She was not slow; she just wasn't getting an education. I still have that report card to wave under administrators' noses when they talk about slow students. I got involved again in Tucson and I went to the first meeting at Tully Elementary and came out the Chairman of the Title One school advisory. Next I went to the district advisory and they sent me on my first plain ride. Yep! All the way to St Louie for the national. I was elected district chairman but I had my hands too full so I gave the seat to someone named Jeanne Miller.

When the Elementary and Secondary Education Act (ESEA) came into Tucson, District One tried to put all whites on the Advisory Board and when the Judge saw this, he ordered more minorities to be appointed. I was put on this important Board representing Tully. We had to explain that it was 98% Hispanics who were affected by desegregation in Tucson and so it was our kids' needs that were to be met because the District was found guilty of segregation. What a battle. All the schools needed help and with Manny Alvarado and Jeannie Ramirez we fought for this help. We had meetings that never ended and it was the first time Hispanic parents were saying "equality."

At this time there was no Bilingual Education Department, there was nothing. With ESEA funds we would ask for everything and hope for the best. Great minds were at work. As we got most of the things we asked for such as teacher aides and materials, we found we had power. We had one Hispanic on the Board and he was the first Chicano ever, Raul Grijalva. He deserves a lot of credit for changing the minds of some very conservative Board members. He was a talking machine and the mover. We were a good team.

At the same time we had the battle going to keep Davis Elementary open. They were trying to tear it down. With the Youth Development Association's help, we started Padre Unidos and I was Chairman and Irene Echeverria along with Juanita Cortez put together workshops for parents and explained about bilingual education and about how we needed Davis to remain open. There were other workshops held by Congreso Nacional De Asunto Colegiales (CONAC) headed by Pepe Baron and his Tucson partner, Hank Oyama. Eva Price was irreplaceable as a leader at Pima College and she along with Hank helped us to organize parent workshops. This gave us the tools to teach the parents about bilingual education and their rights as far as Title One funds. We had a lot of cooperation then, with buses picking up parents at different schools and getting them there. They were paid to attend – one hundred dollars from CONAC - and we provided babysitting. Parents began to understand that having two languages was something to be proud of. It was difficult getting parents to accept bilingual education. They thought "we are in the United States and we want our children educated in English so they can speak English. We don't want them speaking Spanish." We had to let them know our kids could handle both. We had to get them away from the thinking of the 1940's and to show them that the language is slowly disappearing. A black-eyed young lady joined us then by the name of Gloria Limon and she and I would become partners in the fight for equal education.

CHAPTER FORTY-SEVEN: MAMA'S DEATH

This was in 1979 and Mama had not been feeling well. Josie and I became close again when I moved to Tucson. I guess it was because I didn't have to see Ben destroying her. Sonny was working for the City of Tucson and my kids were growing up fine. Josie would come down to Tucson with my Mom and they would visit and we would all go up to Los Angels and visit them too. We always stayed at Josie's and when we got there we would all stay up all night drinking and talking about what had been going on in our lives. Ben, Josie said, had to go to South America because of something or other. I won't go into specifics but I knew it was B.S. We had become close once more and it felt good. My kids and Sonny would go to bed about two a.m. and we would follow about five a.m. Josie was still gullible.

Flashback to 1974: I was awakened one morning with a phone call from my nephew Rudy, Josie's son, telling me that Damon had died. Damon was Josie's youngest son, only 6 years old. "How?" I said.

"I don't know, Auntie Nellie, please come."

"Where is your mother?"

"Right here with the police."

"Put her on the phone."

"Hurry Auntie Nellie."

"Josie, what happened?"

"I don't know, he just died."

"I'll be right there."

"Okay." We talked about that conversation for years because I said, "I'll be right there" and it seemed to her like I was around the corner. That was in 1974/75. Damon was the same age as Christy and of the two; Damon was big and healthy looking while Christy was small and always sick. I was sure someone had left drugs or something around and he got them. Rudy kept saying no. I thought, I'll find out when I get to Los Angeles. At that time I did not fly on airplanes; I didn't care what was happening, I didn't fly. We packed the car and we headed to Los Angeles and at this time it took forever because Phoenix was not fixed up as it is now and you had to go through all these little towns. Sonny drove like a maniac, bless him. When we pulled up it was dusk and everyone was there, including Ben. Boy that was a fast trip from South America. Josie was drunk and no tears. "What happened?" It seemed that Josie had awakened in the night when she heard bumping and when she went into Damon's room he was in a convulsion. She held him and Rudy and Benny Jr. were all screaming and calling the police. Josie said he looked at her and she saw the light leave his eyes. Benny Jr. ran outside in his underwear screaming and threw himself down in the driveway just screaming. I don't know where Lainnie, Josie's daughter was. Rudy called me.

I went with Ben to the funeral home and made arrangements. Josie was given a shot by a doctor and she was out of it. She kept crying all night. He was six and had never been sick. Ben sat in a chair all night. As I slept, I heard Josie scream and then she was running to me. I was in the back bedroom with Sonny and my girls.

Ben was right behind her. She showed me a picture screaming all the while and when I looked it was of Ben and his girlfriend making love. Polaroid. Ben took it from me and he said he was going home. Josie said, "You are home." He left. I stayed as long as I could and I hated to leave my sister alone. Mom moved in with her; I thought Mom could help her. My heart breaks to this day when I think of the next call from Mom. Josie had been taken to the hospital. They said she was standing on her porch in the night screaming "someone help me." They took her into the psychiatric ward at the General Hospital. She then went into convulsions. Where was Ben?

Josie made it with my Mom's help; it was a full time job. Josie needed to work. Ben didn't support her or the kids and she was about to lose her house. Mom gave her money for the house but it was not enough. I went up there and together with a lot of pep talks we sent Josie off for her first job interview. She got the job. Meanwhile we got the certificate of death for Damon. Lymphoid Leukemia. No warning. It does happen that way. Maybe he was lucky he didn't suffer. He was sick for just a few days with flu-like symptoms.

We really got close but it was still good I lived in Tucson. Josie really drank and Mom along with her. I would go up for visits and Junior, Fud, Bud and their wives would come over to Josie's and we would sing. Roberta, Junior's wife, was just like us. I still feel like she was raised in the Gardens. When I would be at Josie's, all the girls would stop by. Yes, we all were still close and no one lived too far. Bernie was still always with Josie and Vicky along with Dory and Jolly. They would come over and talk about old times.

Josie had been calling me telling me Mom was sick but she would go to her Doctor and he kept saying it was old age,or she had a light touch of jaundice soon to clear up with his magic pill. The time she called me and was crying she said that Mom was getting worse and she was not going to take the blame if she went in her room and she was dead. I told her" take her to the General, she loves that place."

When the call came that Mom was sick and that they were going to operate I knew somehow that this was it. I remember it was in May of 1980; I went up to be with Josie. Annette was graduating from Tucson High School, so my kids stayed behind to finish out the school year and Sonny drove me up to Los Angeles. Josie said she needed surgery. When I got to the hospital, Mom was being brought to her room from x-rays. She was yellow! I mean her eyes and skin and she looked awful. I gave her a kiss and Sonny couldn't keep the look off his face and Mom just gave him her hand. She was to have surgery the next morning and Annette was to graduate in two nights. Sonny planned to leave after the surgery so he at least would be at Annette's graduation. That night I slept with Josie and I had a dream that Mom had cancer. When I woke up I told Josie and she said nonsense. I knew. Sonny left us at the hospital and when my brothers came we all waited. When she came out of surgery it was late. Junior and Fud had left to be with their families after being assured that Mom was all right. When I saw the doctor I went up to him and asked him point blank if she had cancer. Josie pinched me. He looked at us and with a tired expression said, "Yes." Josie and I told him thank you and he let us know she had about six months. It was cancer of the pancreas. We found a corner in the hallway that was dark and held each other and cried.

When we went back to Josie's house, Sonny had gone for a trailer to take some things we had stored at Josie's house back to Tucson with him. He walked into the house and Josie and I told him and he held us. He took the trailer back and headed home. He brought the kids back with him and I was so sad to have missed Annette's big moment. After Mom's surgery they said she might need blood and sent us all downstairs to give. Me!!! No,no. I have rolling vains I said as they tested my blood. But it's Mom. Ok, but please be gentle. They hooked Josie up and then very gently put the needle in my arm and then they had to try again. Got it. They sat holding my hand and Josie starts getting mad. "If you don't mind my bag is full." Leave it to you Nellie to get all the attention. What am I anyway?" See we never outgrew it. Everyone went to give blood and it was the first time for my kids. Annette fainted in the elevator and we had to sit her down. One thing strange is my Moms blood is A+ and so are all her children. Only my son is A+ and he keeps telling me to behave myself or when I need his blood, he'll have to think it over. Annette stayed with me in Los Angeles; she wanted to be with me to help with her Nana. Everyone else went home to Tucson. We got a hospital bed and now Josie worked for the phone company so Annette and I, along with Josie's daughter Lorraine, stayed home and took care of Mom while Josie worked. We were a team. I went back and forth on the train and then Annette would go back to Tucson for a while. I think Annette would have made a good nurse. She did things I couldn't do. It was hard and Mom was very weak. Josie and I tried to give her morphine for the pain but she kept saying she wanted to save it for the big pain. Bernie and my cousin Terry were always there. My brother Junior drove me home to Tucson one time in his Volkswagen van. We would crawl up the hills and all the cars would pass us. He would shake his fist at them and say "I'll get you, laugh at me will you?!" Going downhill was a different story. We flew. He is the funniest man I know.

When I got to Tucson, Irene, Gloria Limon would come over and we would discuss what was happening as far as Davis, ESEA and we would plan what they would do. When I was in Tucson I would try to do as much as possible. I was part of an interviewing panel along with Gene Benton and Marybelle McCorkle, when the call came that Mom was real bad. I called Gene and told him my choice and I caught the train that night. Gene and Irene came to the station to say good-bye. I took Annette with me. When we got there, Mom was not that bad but I knew Josie was scared and she needed me. She had no one to help her. Lainnie was always out and on drugs.

All the time we took care of Mom, she had a bell that she would ring all night long for everything. I hated that bell. We always went though and got her water or whatever.

I think many times she was just scared. I would leave her light on. Josie snored like no one I have ever heard. I mean loud. When it was time to go to sleep I would beg her to please let me go to sleep first. I tried a radio pillow and earplugs and nothing worked. She also had a cat that would come in the window at my head and scare me to death. One night Lainnie came in late and was feeling no pain; I slept in a twin bed in Josie's room, and she goes to wake Josie and I sit up. She sees me and it is dark. She screams, Josie sits up, Lainnie screams again. I scream. Josie screams. Lainnie lands on the floor. It was a comedy like the three stooges. Another time Josie left for work and I slept late. Mom did not wake me. I went to her room and looked in and she was just lying there. No movement. I couldn't see her take a breath. I called Josie home from work. She looks at Mom and we stand at the end of her bed just staring. All of a sudden she opens her eyes and we scream. We had been sure she was dead. I don't know why they do it, but they kept making us take Mom in for appointments. By then the Doctor had told us she knew she was dying. She was so weak it was torture. She went all the way down to 89 lbs and she looked weak.

Now every time I came back she knew Josie had called me cause she was worse. The last time I entered the house I felt like a shadow of doom. She looks at me and says"shit I'm worse". My Mom did not cuss.

When the day did come, Mom woke us with moans and we gave her her morning drink of Ensure and she threw it up. "Now what the hell is going on," she said. Now she was in real pain. Josie and I are like two animals. We have to go to the laundry to do the wash. This is because we must make our plan. We leave Annette and Lainnie to take care of Mom. She is not awake. While at the Laundromat we decide that it has now come to the question of mercy killing. I said no. She pinched me and pulled my finger. All this at the laundromat with people looking. I wanted to call my brothers but we knew they would call an ambulance. The doctor had told us if we called and she had one breath in her, they must put her on life support. She didn't want that. That is one of the reasons she chose to die at home. When we got home you could hear her moaning all through the house. "Okay Josie, your way." We went into her room and I got the morphine pills and she was delirious and told us she had a dream and in it the family home in Tucson on 22nd Street was filled with her family. They were sitting on the porch. I had never heard of a house on 22nd Street. I gave her two pills and Josie mixed them with water and made a paste so she could swallow them. She wanted her Saint lit and after lighting it she kept saying Mary. She held first Josie's hand then mine and we rubbed her back. Annette took over and we rested and then said we should call the boys. Bud got there, Junior and Roberta got there, and she talked to them with the door closed. Josie and I knew the morphine was working because for the first time she was out of pain.

We paged Fud and he had to drive across Los Angeles to get there and when he comes in we tell him it is time, and he said, "call the ambulance, she looks awful." We all rush into her room and her eyes are up. "She didn't look like that earlier, I guess she waited for you," I tell Fud. We circle her bed and I just rubbed her head and she looked at us as her breath left her. I went down to the floor and we all cried. Annette was hysterical. I went to her but nothing helped. She did manage to call Tucson and let my son know her Nana had passed away and it was time for them to come. She was then hysterical again and we gave her a sedative to calm her down and she slept. We got some beer and called the police and the number Forrest Lawn gave us. We all kept going in to look at Mom. I had closed her eyes and they kept opening. Junior said she was still watching us. Josie and I went to the kitchen and hugged. Mom would be proud of us. The cops came and they look at us like "where are the tears?" They don't know how many tears we had cried for six months. Then they say they must have an autopsy performed. Josie and I run into the kitchen. What are we to do? No one else knew. What would our brothers say? Would we go to jail? Oh God. Our families. Forrest Lawn gets there and they make a phone call and it's cleared. You see, we had made arrangements long before and so the doctor knew she wanted to die at home. Then we found out she was supposed to be taking two tablets of morphine every four hours. We didn't kill her. Oh God, thank you. I sure am glad Mom had died on her own accord. She didn't want a priest so I did ask her if she was sorry for all her sins and she said yes. I made the sign of the cross on her head.

Mom had a beautiful service at Forrest Lawn at the Wee Kirk Chapel and they played Lieberstrauss and Fud read "Do Not Weep For Me For I Am Not There." All the old families attended and she had the best we could afford. After the service, Josie said, "Mom would have liked it. Too bad she wasn't here." I told you we were crazy after six months.

CHAPTER FORTY-EIGHT: DEALING WITH BILINGUAL EDUCATION

Back at home we were dealing with Davis Bilingual Elementary School and we started the long process of the principal ship. Oh yes, the school was ours. There was a big meeting held at the Board of Education building in Tucson to vote on the establishment of Davis and on the school board were many people opposed both to bilingual education and to keeping Davis open. This movement was lead by Eva Bacal and So Ling Tom. "No, No," she kept saying and poor Raul Grijalva and Laura Almquist kept trying to turn her around. Comes the night of the meeting we packed the Boardroom with all brown people. It was beautiful. Irene went on Ernesto Portillo's radio program and explained to the parents in Spanish about the vote. I picked up many parents in my van and took them to the meetings. Cruz Martinez could talk to the older ladies and get them moving when no one else could. When I had all the ladies in the van, it was only about two inches off the ground. Now I'm not saying they weighed a lot, but they were healthy.

When the van door opened at the Board and all these women fell out, it scared the hell out of the Board. Gloria and Juanita went door to door near Davis to get those ladies out. So Long Tom (as we called him) and Eva changed their vote and we got our very first victory. Raul called me later that night and when I answered the phone all he said was "thanks" and hung up. That's Raul, a man of few words when he is moved.

I actually realized how important bilingual education was when I was working with Spanish- speaking students in Los Angeles and I couldn't communicate. In a way it helped the students because I would tell them I was *tonta*. You teach me, I'll teach you. I guess it was a form of bilingual education. They didn't think they were stupid. The language is a precious gift of inheritance and I was robbed of it. This is the gift I want to give the children. Parents don't realize that as each generation goes by, the children are losing their inheritance and culture. They are getting lazy with the language and they will end up like me and you don't want this to happen. Well, I speak zoot suit Spanish!

Some of the obstacles come because there's still discrimination and misunderstanding of us as a people. It comes from people who are insecure and are looking for a victim to blame their shortcomings on. I know because of my attitude; I thought something was wrong with me because I was dark. I had a complex that stayed with me until I realized I was a great beauty (ha, ha, a joke).

With the help of CONAC, I got the feel of education again and so I entered Pima Community College where I majored in pre-education and I found I loved learning. I became a member of Phi Theta Kappa and transferred to the University of Arizona. I was now into History as my major and Political Science as my minor. I wanted to go into secondary education because I had hated History when I was in high school and it was boring. I wanted to teach History in its true form and also teach Chicana History like Dr. Raquel Rubio Goldsmith and Lupe Castillo. What a pair of strong women. They make our history interesting and are a good example of it.

I remember the first day I entered the University. It was 7:30 a.m. and the sun was already hot. It was a summer course so hardly anyone was around. I was walking to the Science Building and the tower rang out the time and sang its little song. I thought, "who would have ever thought I would be here." I had become a grandmother and I was at the University. It must be a dream. My granddaughter, Stefanie Angela Pesqueira, was born June 15, 1981. I remember thinking life was good. Stefanie has now graduated from Northern Arizona University and lives in Chandler with her own family. Ryan and Conner. Yep I am a great grandmother. She did graduate from Tucson High School and has gone through the bilingual strain. I now have nine going on ten grandchildren and seven are bilingual and play mariachi music. They write and read Spanish and can carry on a conversation. Yes, I am very pleased.

I went back and forth to Los Angeles to visit. Josie, now alone, was very successful at the phone company and was the Operations Administrator. She was good at her job and was liked by all her co-workers. She worked for Ma Bell. Her kids were still with her and Benny Jr., who had been her biggest headache, met his future wife Linda and got off drugs and became a Jehovah's Witness. Her son Rudy worked and Lainnie slept and did drugs. She had a son with her boyfriend Peter and together they tried to ruin their son's life. Thank God for grandparents. Josie took over his support and rearing. She lived for her grandson Justin. Josie and I had grandsons born just weeks apart and so when we would visit each other, they played and were very close. Rudy, Josie's son, took care of Justin and was very close to him also. He called Rudy "Lala". It looked as if Josie had someone to live for. Rudy Torres Josie's son is a well know Chicano artist. Bernie, Terry, and Jolly all stayed close in friendship with Josie and all had a bond that went way back. Me too. I would go up to Los Angeles and we would party until the wee hours of the morning. We sang "In the Still of the Night" just as we did in the Gardens. We would talk about old times and what each of us was doing. Bernie was into insurance, Josie was at the phone company and Terry owned a beauty shop in Alhambra called Talk About Hair. We would all have our hair done and it would take a whole day because we yacked so much. Bernie now had a grandson whom she could spoil and Josie had hers; I had my five grandchildren, Terry had none. I was expecting one from my daughter Annette in February 1991. It was David and Annette's first child. We had waited a long time for this. Suzette had two, Christy had two, and Rudy (my son) had one. Annette and David had a hard time getting pregnant. I had three good son-in-laws and all my girls had careers and good kids and they all loved their Nana. Life was good. We had all reached a point in our lives where we could fly (I got over my fear of flying) and Sonny and I were traveling.

CHAPTER FORTY-NINE: TWO BARRIO KIDS IN EUROPE

We went to Europe in 1985 and stayed with some friends in Germany. Arlene and Bill put us up in their house in Manheim and Arlene, my best friend in Tucson, and I had many similar likes as far as history. It was something I never would have believed could happen to me.

I remember on the plane, Sonny got my hand and said, "Would you believe two kids from a barrio would be on a plane to Europe?" "No, I wouldn't," I said. I loved Europe and when we went to Florence and I saw Michelangelo's tomb next to Dante's, I cried. History was all over the place. In Rome, people had columns in their front yards from the past and were so non-chalant about it. We sat across the street from Mussolini's window where he made all his speeches and made bets if the pedestrians would make it across the street. People drive crazy there. I went to the Vatican and saw Michelangelo's Sistine Chapel. No words are needed or can be used to describe my feelings.

Sonny loved Germany and the beer. I thought his nose would explode with all the beer he drank. This I'm sure was his paradise.

Arlene and I, as we always, got into mischief and had a lot of fun. Example: In Rome we went to an Italian Restaurant for dinner and they had two musicians playing. Well as you finish your glass of wine, they keep filling it. Wine flows like water there. We start singing "Sabor Ami" and then we all walked to the Tivoli Fountain ("Three Coins in the Fountain") singing "Arriva Derrchi Roma." I will return.

So as you can see I just kept moving on with life's adventures. I had my educational involvement and Sonny had his life. I was on all sorts of Boards and won't go into all of them. The one involvement that was the most important of my life was being a plaintiff in a suit against the school district in Tucson that took eight years of my life. We had to show unequal education and we did. The sad part was the other plaintiffs were Anglo. No Chicanos. This was for our kids. A lot of Chicanos were scared of upsetting the apple cart and thank God they weren't in East Los Angeles with the movement. We proved our case and won.

We worked with Dr. Macario Saldate and others to provide bilingual teachers for our District. He was a shaker at the University. He had to fight hard for the Mexican American Center. He was the first director and a tribute to the Hispanics in Tucson. All this and Los Angeles too.

I kept going back to school and every time I did something would happen in the family that took me out again. I still plan to go back and maybe graduate with my granddaughter. Now I have eight grandchildren and I think that is my career. In today's world, everyone has to work in order to buy a home and pay for education. I give my grandchildren the home base. They come home from school and hit the old refrigerator. Big house now, pool table, big television and lots of Love. They are like brothers and sisters. The oldest is a Junior at Tucson High School and I am so proud of her. My Stefanie Pesqueira. All my grandchildren are bright, well thought of students, and I am so proud of them. The best part is they are CHICANO and they know it. Hopefully this will be the generation that does it. I have been saying that for too long.

CHAPTER FIFTY: MY SISTER IS DYING

Here I am on a plane headed for Los Angeles, January 4, 1992. Rain is beating down on the plane window and people are talking and laughing. I want to scream "Shut up, don't you know my sister is dying?" Was it just a year ago when I got that horrible call? I was home and it was early morning on the morning of January 30, 1991. "Hey Nellie, you wouldn't believe what happened to me."

"Now what?" I reply.

"Well last night, I started bleeding and it wouldn't stop so I drove over to the hospital and they said I was hemorrhaging. They took some tests and they'll call me tomorrow."

"What did they say it was?" I'm getting scared now.

"Oh don't worry, it's nothing, you know me." I do know her and that is why I'm scared.

"Josie, have you been getting your pap tests?" a sinking feeling is in the pit of my stomach.

"Well, I have missed a few." I knew it.

"Josie, how long?"

"None of your business, I've been going almost every year. Besides I'm an adult and I don't have to answer to you."

"Have you been to your doctor lately, Miss Smarty Pants?"

If there is one thing I have learned about my wayward sister is that she is always on defense. When you have her in a corner, she will attack.

This is always Josie's defense. Attack. "Josie, this is important, how long?"

"About five years, but don't worry, I'm okay, honest." I told her to call me when she heard from the doctor. I threw up. I knew it was cancer.

I tried to keep busy the next day and not think about it. Her face was always in front of me. I had a meeting at Nosotros, a neighborhood agency headed by my friend Frank Romero. I told my son and husband to call me when Josie called. I was in the meeting with Manny Alvarado, Bill Morris, the lawyer, and Frank when the phone rang and I could feel my hands trembling. "Nellie, it's for you."

My son said, "Come home, Auntie Josie called and wants you to call her." I had told the guys that I was expecting this call so I just looked at them and said, "gotta go." When I got home I called Josie and she said the doctor had called her and not to worry. It was cancer and she was to go to a specialist at the General Hospital Cancer Center. We both kept up a chitter chatter but it was a false talk. I told her I would go with her and she said my sister-in-law Roberta had called and would be going too.

"Great, we can make a day of it. I'll take the plane out and be in Los Angeles on the first." Her appointment was on the second. I put down the phone and screamed. "Not again! I hate cancer!" My husband and son tried to console me but nothing helps when you are in your own hell. I called the airlines and made a reservation for the first at 1:30 p.m. and started packing. The phone rings again and it's

Annette. She is in labor and comes to my house after leaving work early. Off I go to be with her at her house as her labor continues. She took all night and kept arguing with me about her labor. She would politely call the doctor and tell her she was having pains. "First one, it will take some time" the doctor tells her. I told her her water broke and she had to go in. Oh no, she knew better. I made her go and her husband David was so scared you would have thought it was him having the baby.

At 3:30 a.m. Annette walked through the lobby at University Medical Center with her legs crossed. "Hurry, hurry." She had had nightmares about not getting there in time for her epidural. The doctor on duty examined her and tells her she is in early labor, just beginning. I stayed with her and then at about 4:00 a.m., I went to the waiting room to get some sleep. "Hurry, it's time," David is yelling.

"Oh thank God it's time for the epidural."

"No, she's having the baby!" David yells. It was 7:30 a.m. and I'm up and in her room faster than a speeding bullet. She is in hard labor and she tells me it's like her dream. It was too late to give her an epidural. I just kept praying because she was in pain. Please let it be over. A baby's scream. "A girl." I have seen many babies born including all my grandchildren, but never have I seen such a tiny baby. She was long with these long hairy arms and legs, both thin, and her hands and feet were big. Her hair ran down her face to her eyebrows. Hair everywhere. The cry was different, it sounded more like a cat. This was my Desiree. She is now five and beautiful. She turned cute when she turned one month. When they put her in the baby warmer she kept slinking around.

Annette had a bad time and I stayed with her until nine and my oldest daughter picked me up and took me home. I called Josie and told her the baby was here. I'm going to get some sleep and be there at 4:00 p.m. Pick me up at the airport. I did sleep and when I woke I was both happy and sad. I called Annette and left for the airport with Sonny. "She is probably exaggerating." I just looked at him.

Did he know I wanted to hit someone? No, I don't think so. When I got into Los Angeles, Josie and Roberta were there to meet me. We kept talking as if this was just a precautionary step. When we got to Josie's, we drank, smoked and talked as we always did. I don't know about Josie, but that night as I slept next to her, I knew that tomorrow would hold disastrous news. She still snored and I didn't mind that much. I found out that she had been hemorrhaging badly and there was no one home to take her to the hospital. She just made it, she was so weak. I was mad. Where was Lainnie? I knew Rudy had been at work. We had to find Lainnie so she could take care of her son the next morning. Roberta comes for us and off we go with nerves on edge. "There is a parking space."

"No not there."

"Shut up."

"Oh yeah." In we go and you can smell cancer. People are there without hair and some look like they are already dead. The children get to me and it is hard not to cry when they talk to you. They call Josie in and we all go. "No, you two wait here," the nurse says. "Okay, okay, we'll be right out here Jo, call us when you're done."

The doctor examines her and then she gets dressed and calls us in. "Well, it's cancer of the cervix. It is in stage one but I don't like the size of it," the doctor says. "What I would like to recommend is radiation to shrink it and then remove it surgically."

"That's it?"

"Yes, I would recommend it to my mother if she had it."

"Oh Josie, you're going to be all right."

"Sure," she says. "I told you it was nothing to worry about." This is really the way she thinks. Josie always thought that she was invincible. I used to bawl her out because she wouldn't go to the dentist. She would rather have a baby then go to the dentist. She would pop her abscess with a pin to keep from going. She hated to have a pap smear because when we were young, she always had to go back for follow-ups and she hated them looking at her. Now everyone was looking at her. We would kid her with "open wide." She didn't laugh. We set up her appointment with Dr. Rose and he is nice. He agrees with the other doctor and sets up her radiation treatment at Huntington Memorial. I take her for her treatments twice a week and she made me laugh describing how this young man must have her buck naked on a bed so he can draw a cross where the radiation goes. She was heavyset and he had trouble, to her delight. I now am driving all over in her little beat-up car. She says she will get a new car when this is all over.

She wants to go to work but the doctor won't release her. I still don't' understand that. She was well and she loved her job. She was bored without it. She got the same amount on her check, I guess it was some kind of insurance from work. Her friends from work would stop by the house to see her. Oh how she missed them. One in particular, Irma and her husband, had been like a brother and sister to her when I was gone. They would fix things for her and take her out. They didn't mind that she drank too much. They loved Josie for herself. She was Elizabeth Taylor in "Who's Afraid of Virginia Wolf."

When she drank she was obnoxious just like my dad. He had died a few years after my mom and I didn't go to the funeral. Josie had some satisfaction when my Father had come looking for my Mom again. She said, "Sure go down on Glendale and make a right at the cemetery. You can find her there." I wish I had been there.

After two months of treatment, including the insertion of two metal balls into her vagina and a hospital stay, you couldn't stay longer than two minutes because of the exposure. Of course Bernie, Terry, and I had a lot of jokes at her expense. She looked like nothing was wrong. When they took out those balls they almost rip you open. They told her to think it's like having a baby. I went in after they were through and they said she did well. The doctor said the tumor had shrunk and now all they had to do was take it out. Now

Josie, who always knew she would be fine, was sneaking drinks. I would wonder why she would sit at home watching television and drink glass after glass of water. It was white wine. When she got home this time, I caught on and told her I was going home because if she didn't want to get well I was not wasting my time with her. She promised me she would stop. I kept catching her and finally one night, I cleaned out her hiding place, which I found that day, and threw out all the beer and wine. There were two doors in her bathroom, one in the hall across from her room and one in the back porch that led to the kitchen. What she had been doing was acting like she was going to the bathroom as I watched television in the front room, and I heard her being sneaky. Now that I knew, I heard the door opening in the kitchen. She tried to tip toe and open the refrigerator quietly, but I could hear and was just pretending I was watching television. She slams the cupboard door and then slams the door to the bathroom. Now she slams the door to the bathroom in the hallway and if looks could kill, I'd be dead.

You want to play games? Fine. I'm leaving tomorrow. I called and made my reservation and she was sheepish when she took me to the airport. I told her I was homesick anyway. I now had two daughters expecting. Suzette after eight years and Christy. "Oh go take care of them. I'm only going in to take the garbage out." It was Easter that weekend and I called to wish her a happy Easter. Rudy tells me that she is Drunk "get her to the phone" I tell him.

"What do you want?" she slurred.

"Josie, what is wrong with you? You need help." She hangs up. She finally passed out and I tell Rudy to put her to bed and then have her call me when she wakes up. She does and says she is sorry.

The next day was her appointment to have her pre-op work done. She calls me screaming that when they took her x-ray they found some cancer. "Come back Nellie, I'm scared."

"I'll be right there." We both start to laugh. I said that before. She picked me up at the airport and on the way to her house, I lecture her.

I know I shouldn't but I do. Then I remember I told her something that hurt her. I wish I could take it back. I said, "God gave you a second chance and you spit in his face."

She said, "No Nellie, I was just scared." Well, we didn't know how bad it was and they had set up an appointment with Dr. Chang, an oncologist next to the Huntington Memorial. I, along with Lainnie, went with Josie that dreadful day. The doctor called her in and we all go. He asked her questions and then tells us to wait outside because he had to examine her. When we are waiting, he came out of the room and motioned us to his office. There he laid it on us. She was terminal and it was up to God when she would go. I was in shock and just stood there. I had known it had spread, but now a new word was added to my vocabulary, metastasis. It was now in five ribs and it had only been in two the week before. He said it was an aggressive cancer.

He left us in his office and went back to Josie. I picked myself up, dusted myself off, and went in as if nothing had happened. We were not to tell her yet. He would let us know when she had to get her estate in order. He had to tell her it had spread and that he wanted to try chemotherapy on her. I told him to give her a tranquilizer because she looked like she was in shock, too. He did and then he ordered her medicine. Tylenol 3 and tranquilizers. Now she didn't have to drink.

I drove her every couple of weeks to the hospital for her stay. When I would take her in, she looked so healthy they kept trying to put me in. They thought I was the one. She would stay two days and I would take her home. She was not too sick and we went shopping and to the show. Even the park. She lived down Valley Blvd. in El Sereno on Ditman Avenue and we could walk to our park, Lincoln Park. We would remember the dances, meetings, and the swimming pool. Old boyfriends and things we did there.

Like when Angie was getting married we gave her a party at the park. Just girls and we had bought a case of beer. Well, the cops come and we throw the whole case into the lake. Boy someone had a surprise when they drained that park a few years later. We talked about the Plaza De La Raza that is located by the lake. We had been active then and I had represented P.I.C.A. at its dedication. I had met Margo, Eddie Albert's wife. She was a Mexican actress and a beautiful person. She kept calling me c*hica.* Her son Eddie was there and he was still young. Josie and I talked about how we crossed the tracks.

I did talk to her about her memories and what kind she wanted to leave. If she wanted everyone to remember a drunk, keep it up. Or she could start now and stay sober for her grandkids. We kept acting like she was going to make it but we both knew. Long talks and I got her out walking. I loved walking and there is nothing like a walk in L.A. in the Spring. Flowers and stars.

We also attended Sacred Heart Church every Saturday evening and Josie got to know the priest. I talked to him about my parish in Tucson, Saint Margaret's, and that I had sung in the choir for as long as I can remember. I met the couple that sang the mass and they were nice. Their voices blended well. "Seek Ye First" was Josie's favorite and of course "Amazing Grace." After a while you would have thought Josie was a saint. That is how her grandchildren remember her.

I now had my own room, which use to be my mother's, and felt like Josie and I could not get any closer. Her ex-husband, Ben (he filed for the divorce), now sponged off Josie because his wife threw him out. He had my mom's room but he got put away. I felt better having my own room because there is a smell to cancer that once you have smelled it, you will never forget. I had smelled it with my Mom and now Josie had that smell. She would put White Shoulders on and she knew I was still sensitive to the smell. She started coughing and couldn't stop. Into the x-ray room and now it was in her lungs. First one, then the other. It was fast. Cough medicine. Codeine. On the fourth of July, Bernie put together a picnic at a park in Alhambra and we all had a great time. Josie took the opportunity to drink and it was okay. I have a video of the picnic and Josie, along with Bernie, dancing slow. I'm dancing with Bernie's husband Marty and we go into a routine about our teens that is something so dear to our hearts, and I watch it once in a while when I miss Josie. She is smiling and trying to sing "Unforgettable."

Bernie's mom is still alive and Bernie and I walk her home. She outlived Josie and I remember her saying why was it Josie and not her? Here she was in so much pain and she had lived. Why? Esperanza Podovani had arthritis in every joint and at the end was confined to a wheelchair.

At the end of the picnic I go to drive a very high Josie home and we have no gas. We had all said we would meet at Josie's for fireworks. I had had my grandson Rudy with me in L.A. for a visit and he and Justin, born the same month and year, were friends. It was nice because we would watch our grandsons play and walk them to the park. My son, Rudy, had come up to get his son and spend the fourth with me. Well everyone takes off and I had just enough gas to get to the gas station. The only trouble was all the gas stations were closed. I finally found one and I think we went in on fumes.

I had never seen Alhambra so deserted. This is usually the time of day when the traffic is crazy. Even on a holiday. Josie's car was a tank and there was no way we could make it back to her house. We had no way of getting help because no one was home. At least no one was answering the phone. I had this awful feeling we would be walking to Josie's and I knew she couldn't make it.

Oh well. At least she was sober. When you don't drink you can't stand drunk people.

We finally get to Josie's house and there are mariachis. Bernie and Marty had passed them playing on the street outside a bar and paid them to go to Josie's house. Here I was about a half hour late. We dance and sing and I tell my son to get me some brandy. Terry and her future husband get there and I remember Chris giving me two hundred for a trip to Vegas. You see, all the workers from Josie's work had put together a trip to Vegas and we were to leave the next morning. Oh what a great tribute to Josie. I would not interfere with her drinking on the trip. Junior is even going. This is how I got her to bed early. I told her I would let her be wild the next day on the trip.

Early the next morning, we're talking 6:30 a.m., we catch the bus for Vegas. Frankie, an old friend and Jolly's brother, is on the bus. He was the best dancer in Lincoln Heights and could still dance. We would get in line to dance with him. He is the one we used to borrow records from for our dances. Of course without his consent. All the people were nice and Josie, Bernie, and some others sat in the back of the bus drinking to and from Vegas. Junior and I took off on our own. The ride back I slept because we had one more trip to take and I was driving. When we got back to L.A., her co-workers presented Josie with a thousand dollars they had collected for our trip to Oregon. She had good friends at the phone company.

We go to sleep and Josie is in pain. She is now on Tylenol 4 and she takes enough to keep her in shape for the start of the trip. We rent a car and pack it the night before. Josie wants to see her son Benny and his wife Linda in Oregon. I would not deny her anything. She is beginning to look awful. Linda is expecting their second child. We start and Lainnie and Justin are with us. Justin acts good. As we drive up Interstate 5, it is like an adventure. Josie is so thrilled. I drove all day and we stayed at a motel up by Sacramento. Josie is traveling well. I think it was the thought that she was to see her son and his family. Jasmine, Josie's granddaughter, was about two, and she wanted to see her before it was too late. Josie is up with the birds the next morning and off we go.

I drove into Portland and thought how much it had grown. The last time I had been there was with my husband and family on our way to Canada. We got lost. Josie calls Benny and he comes and gets us. It is heartbreaking to see her family around her and Linda trying to be cheerful. His house was right in the middle of trees and greenery. After dinner we sat in the patio and soon I notice that there are cherries on a tree. I guess I never thought they grew on trees.

And so many of them. Of course we had to pick them. I think I had Cherry juice all over my face, umm.

We all leave the next morning for Cannon Beach, a resort community in Oregon. It is where the forest meets the beach. Breathtaking. We got a suite on the beach and enjoyed the visit. A lot of pain for Josie. I would take her to the car so no one knew and she would take her pills and when the pain would subside we would go back in and act, everyone acts, like nothing was wrong. One day I left Josie on the beach with Justin and went to the room. I found Linda and Benny crying and they said Josie looked so bad. "I know but don't act like you notice. She wants this visit so bad." Looking at Josie on the beach playing with her grandchildren, you would not know she was dying. She flopped around with them in the sand and dug holes. I got up early one morning, and was walking on the beach by myself when I noticed people walking out to a big rock on the shore. If you know about tides, you know that the tide comes in at night and after ten in the morning the tide starts going out. By noon you can't reach this rock. It is half under water. When I get there people are exploring caves and there are these ugly moles, I guess with no eyes, running around. I go back and drag Josie out there. "No, No, the tide might come in," she says.

"Come on," I tell her. She humored me and as fast as she could she got me back on shore. "Did you see those things?" I ask.

"Nellie, what is wrong with you, disgusting." There is an island off shore that is actually a tomb. How beautiful. I forget the name of it but it was intriguing. More pain more pills.

Our trip home is sad because we know it is her last trip and the last time she will see her son. She is crying softly in her seat and there is nothing I can do to help her. She is trying to keep up the farce in front of Lennie and Justin. The trip home is exhausting and I think I slept a day away. All this time Terry, Bernie, and I are doing everything we can to make her last year good. Terry is still in denial. We get together and drink, sing, and just do whatever we want because we know it is for the last time.

As I said before, Josie's husband is incarcerated in Bakersfield and he keeps calling Josie to get him out. He calls collect from there and one night he calls and talks to her sweet and when she hung up, she looked like she was thirteen again. She looks at me and says, "He loves me." I didn't say anything to burst her bubble. So now we have to go see him, okay.

Bernie gets Marty's van and off we go one morning. What a trip. When we get there, they call Ben and I'm taken aback by his gray hair. In there he didn't have his dye. Only two at a time can visit him so Bernie and I got first so Josie and Lainnie can go next and stay longer. He asks if it is true and we say yes and he, I think for the first time, knows she is dying and when he sees Josie he is nice. Here we go again with the three stooges. We locked the keys in the van. No help is available and it is getting dark. We did the only thing we could. Cut the screen and forced the window open. Poor Marty. He had to put up with us. We sing "In the Still of the Night."

The next time we hear from Ben I knew he was incapable of feelings. This time when Josie turned to me she says, "even now."

"What is wrong?" I ask.

"He told me not to forget him in my will. I told him I would take care of him. Let him wait. Just wait until he sees I will leave him nothing." She looked so sad. We went to see the lawyer the next day. She knew it was near the end and we talked about what everyone would get. No. I didn't want anything. I did take my Mom's picture albums and old records. That was all I wanted. Josie wanted to leave me money because I had taken a year off from my job but I didn't want anything to remind me of this time. I also know how after a death, people turn into animals.

She wanted to make me administrator of her estate but I told her after it was over I wanted just to leave. Bernie was made administrator and I was given power of attorney for her medical care. She and the lawyer asked me if I could do it. Yes! I knew what she wanted and she was not to be kept alive on machines. DRUGS. That's all. I was given a copy of this so when I would need it, I had it to give to the hospital.

After one of these experiences we would do something crazy like the sleepover at Bernie's house. I wrote a journal of this time. It is included and I hope you find it as touching as I do. This is one night that all our friendships became one and I think it will last the rest of our lives. I only hope I will be this lucky to have such good friends at the end of life's journey.

October 19, 1991

We had a going away party for Josie. Where is she going? We do not know. Her cancer is going through her body like a rotten, sneaky, thief. I call it a thief because it will rob us of a special person. And so we had a going away party.

The party consisted of four very close friends; Bernie who was like a sister to her, Nellie, who was her sister and friend, and Terry, who was her make-believe cousin and friend. Friends of 40 years.

We drank a case of wine while Bernie's husband, Marty, stayed in his room to give us freedom of his home. He knows us and we four are famous for being party animals. Always were and always will be.

We drank, we cried, and we sang. We used the bad word <u>cancer.</u> We talked of our past and we talked of our future

One thing that kept coming up. "What would we do with the void in our gang?"

Terry said, "We should stuff Josie and record her voice and when we get together we can sit her in a chair." I said, "Yes, and as we all go we can add to the group." Hey, we were drunk, what do you expect?

Poor Josie. She is losing her hair and it is in little puffs all around her head. Well, Bernie decides to shave it to make it even.

Right? "Sure" Terry and I say. So Bernie starts to shave it. God I am glad she stopped. One good thing, it is even in the front.

Bernie always gets dramatic and as tears ran down her face she puts a priceless ring on Josie's finger and tells her of her undying love. (When we sobered up Josie gave the ring back, but we made Bernie sweat.)

At about four in the morning we made up the sofa bed and all four of us slept in it. Cuddled together for the last time. I knew it, we all knew it, and we sang. Yep, it's probably the last time we four will sing together. I fell asleep about the time of the fourth version of "In the Still of the Night."

What a way to go!

CHAPTER FIFTY-ONE: THE TIME IS DRAWING NEAR

The time is drawing near and we all know it. Each time Josie is in the hospital it is worse and now she has a gray cast to her coloring. The doctor tells her to get her estate in order. When we leave the office, I tell her to scream if she wants but she says no. She is calm. I am a mess. I want to scream.

The next day Bernie and I go with Josie on the trip of a nightmare. We go to get her coffin and make arrangements for her funeral. We first go to Maribal's on Broadway in Lincoln Heights. Everyone goes there; it's the place to go. When we get there, Josie, who likes to shock people, says to the man, "I'd like to see something in my size." Bernie and I almost died. We are scared and she is joking. He took us upstairs and we looked at all the caskets and she chose a blue one that said, "Going Home." "Yes that will do." Bernie and I are pushing each other by then. Nerves on edge, we continue and sit down with the man to make out the contract. You can tell Josie got him. He was nervous. "I want everything done so I can relax," she says. Oh no, it's the martyr time. He gets so nervous he can hardly hold the pen. With that all done, we go to eat. You want to talk about eating rocks. That's what the meal felt like. By now we are screaming at each other with nerves. "Well, let's go get my grave," Josie says. Oh God! How much more can we take.

To the Resurrection Cemetery we go. It is in San Gabriel. Josie keeps checking us out to see if she is having the effect she wants. There we are. Teeth clinched, sweat on our faces, trying to keep the tears back. She loved it.

When we get there, she leads us into the office. "I called for an appointment," Josie said.

"In one moment," the office girl says.

"Now," said Josie.

"Yes, Mam."

Josie finally got assertive. "Now you two come on," Josie says. We follow like two puppies, our tails between our legs. Josie asks what kind of grave she can get. I ask if we can move her son Damon to her grave.

"No," says the girl.

"Why not?" I ask.

"Don't get excited Nellie, why not?" Josie asks.

"If she wants it why not?" I ask the girl again.

"She just can't," says the girl.

Bernie is still shaking. Josie reaches across and plucks a hair off the outside of my nose. "Where did that come from?" she says.

"I don't know but I don't grow hair on the outside of my nose," I tell her.

"Leave it alone," Bernie says.

"I'll pluck it if I want," Josie says.

"I don't grow hair on the outside of my nose."

The poor lady is just sitting there looking at us like she can't believe it. "Now why can't she have her son moved?" I ask again.

"Just a moment," the girl says as she leaves the room. While she is gone, Josie tells us to behave.

"Us?" Bernie says.

"You're too nervous Nellie. Take a tranquilizer," Josie says.

"I am not, you take one," I tell her.

"I did," says Josie.

"Well then give me one."

In comes the woman. "I did check and the reason we can't move Damon is because he had no bell (protector) and all that is left is dirt. Do you want us to move that?" the girl says…what a smart ass. We all just look at her with our mouths open. She has a smile.

"No, that's okay." Bitch. Now we go in the lady's car and she takes us on a tour. First grave, no too crowded. Second, no scenery. Third, just right. Up on top of a hill. Josie checked her neighbors. Yes, they looked okay.

Now she stood at the end of her grave and looked over her shoulders. "Yes it seems to fit, I'll take it." Now Bernie and I are just holding on to each other. I think we would have fallen if we let go. That done we return to the office and we are in shock for the rest of the day. When we get to Josie's, I feel sick.

We keep going to the doctor's and she goes in for her chemo treatment and she just keeps looking worse. I decide to go home for the holidays. I knew Josie was in good hands with Bernie and Terry taking care of her. The friendship is as one. I go home for Thanksgiving and as usual, my brother Junior and his wife Roberta and their kids come down for the holiday. This has been for many years and I hope it will continue for many more years. Josie comes down to Tucson with her son Rudy and daughter Lainnie and Justin; everyone is glad. This way they get to see her. Suzette and Christy are far along in their pregnancies and can't travel. My grandchildren loved their Auntie Josie with the "Flintstones feet." That's just one thing she showed with pride. We use to call them hamburger feet. She was gray and had shadows under her eyes. Her cough was continuous and she was always in pain.

When she left she hugged the girls good-bye and we all knew it was the last time. My son-in-laws hugged her and as she took off, I told her I would be up right after New Year's. I can still see her eyes as she took off, looking back.

When we were thanking God for all he had done for us, Josie just said, "We have to talk" as she looked up. That is Josie, take her or leave her.

Christmas comes and there is sadness mixed with the joy of Christmas and little children's laughter. I was home but my mind was with Josie. She was taking longer to recuperate from the chemotherapy and she could hardly talk. She called me New Year's Eve and said, "Have a wonderful year, Nellie." Her voice was a whisper. I can still hear her. "I'll be up there in a few days, Josie, I leave the seventh, hang in there." I remember drinking my coke and brandy that night and looking at the tree of memories. The lights flashing and taking me back to so many Christmas's before. Well, Happy New Year Josie…sure.

On January fourth I got a call from Bernie. She was hysterical.

"What?"

"She had a car wreck and she is in Huntington Memorial," she says.

"How did it happen Bernie?" I ask.

"She was driving her car and had some kind of attack."

"What the hell was she doing driving?"

"I'll be right there," I tell her. Again I made my reservation and here I am on my way back to see the ending of this life. God give me strength. It was pouring as I came down in Burbank. You could hardly see outside the window. As I leave the plane, I spot the two of them crying. Terry grabs my bag and Bernie grabs me. We start talking all at once. Get calm. Okay now what happened? Lorraine, Lainnie, had been out the night before and some guys came to the front door looking for her. They just walked in. Rudy was in the back painting. He is a known painter and he had his earphones on. The guy pushed Josie to the floor and took her VCR. She crawls to Rudy's room and he finally hears her. Too late, the punks are gone.

The next morning was Josie's appointment, the fourth, and no one was there to take her. She lied to Terry and said she had a ride. Terry would call every day to make sure she didn't need something. Josie doesn't wait and takes off for the hospital. She couldn't leave Justin with Lorraine because she didn't know what she would do. So Josie, too proud to ask Terry, drives herself to the doctor's. Lorraine and Justin are with her. On the way she turns blue and has an attack. She hit a tree with her car. No one else was seriously hurt but Josie's leg was smashed.

As we drive through the night, I just keep thinking *Josie wait for me*. When we get to the hospital, it is dark. Bernie and Terry had noticed earlier that a back door to the hospital was left open. They were not casing the joint but they had good training (joke). We go in and sneak up the elevators to her room. There she is. She is still alive. The first thing she says is "I know, you told me not to drive."

"See what happens if I leave you on your own," I answer.

"Please don't scold me now."

"Well you should have known better." There is a woman in the bed next to her and Josie is in the broken bones part of the hospital. The doctor will not be in until the morning so I don't know if the attack was the disease or just an accident. We all stayed late and Junior is calling Linda and making arrangements for her to get down here from Alaska. I remember going back to Josie's house and it was raining. Her house was empty. I slept for a few hours and the phone rings and it is Junior. He will be picking up Linda. Lorraine calls from the hospital and an Aunt was trying to have them disconnect Josie's morphine. I called the desk and told them I had the power of attorney for Josie's medical needs and I wanted them to give her as much as possible. They agree and that problem is solved. I shower and get ready. Terry comes for me and Bernie is to meet us at the hospital.

When I get there a priest comes into the room and gives her the last rites. She is still fully conscious and the nurse goes to take her temperature just when the priest is going to take her confession. I don't know how much Josie paid her but it looked planned to me. This is going to be the confession of all confessions so Bernie grabs a paper and pencil and I lean forward to hear and talk about luck, he says, "I know it is hard for you to talk, so are you sorry for all your sins?" Josie nods and has that laugh in her eyes. Bernie, the nurse, Josie and I join hands with the priest and say the Our Father and Hail Mary. He asks if she wants him back the next day and she nods yes. She has a tube in her nose for air. Terry had to go back to work so we stay all day. Everyone comes to see her. All the girls and relatives. My cousin Freddie jokes with her and then Linda gets there. Josie is having those attacks and turns blue. I have to massage her chest to get her breathing again. The nurse had shown me how. It was the disease that had now gone into her brain. They couldn't operate on her leg because of the lungs having cancer. She was in great pain and still she was the ham with all her company. The doctor told me to give her a lot of morphine because she was in so much pain. Josie was determined to visit all her company so I would sneak the button that controls the morphine and when it would make a beeping noise she would look at me and say, "What is that?"

"Nothing," I told her.

She knew I was up to something. She had the room packed and the nurse moved the other woman out to another room. Josie is flying now and the company leaves. Even Jeanette is there. Linda goes to Josie's house to rest after her plane ride. It takes about eight hours to make the trip. She had stayed with Josie for a while during Josie's illness and they had that time together. Now it is night and Terry returns. Bernie and I decide to stay over and Terry agrees. We had a pajama party in her room with singing and Bernie had her El Presidente in her coffee. We had Josie right in the middle of it all and when I asked her if she was stoned she said, "Yeah." You see, we had our last conversation with her. She was going under with the morphine and she sang and asked me to sing "Be-Bop Wino" to her "new room." The doctor came to talk to us. He motioned Linda and me out and Bernie went too. In the hallway he stood there and looked like he was going to cry and told us this was the end. We start to laugh. We gave him a hug and told him we knew. I felt so sorry for him. I think he never had met someone like Josie before and he liked her. Example: When the doctor told Josie he wanted more x-rays, she insisted on a mammogram.

"Why?" he asked.

"Well I have my image to uphold." Her other famous line to him was, "I lived by my twat and I'll die by my twat." He was Chinese and short and a very serious man and Josie could get him laughing. I put a rosary I got at the Vatican over her head on a bar. Now began the long wait. Josie was now out of it. Linda and I stayed with her until the end. We slept in chairs and Bernie brought us a care package with a change of clothes. People came and went and the priest stopped by every day and we would tell her to let go. During this time she came to and said, "Nellie, I'll come for you." "Not for a long time Jo," I said. Her son Benny and his wife had arrived on the second day so she had said her good-byes to everyone. We had thought that that was what she was waiting for but no, she just didn't want to go and nobody was going to make her go.

The doctor gave me tranquilizers because my heart was acting up. I have a heart murmur and it was going all over. I even scared myself. Waiting is worse than the death but I think it is God's way of setting the stage. By the time it comes, you are glad it is over.

The night Josie died it was raining and the room was still with solemn people just in their own hell. Benny said he had to get back to Oregon and Rudy was next to Josie by the side of the bed. Linda and I had gone to Josie's to shower and had left Bernie with Josie. When we got back we could hear singing and talking from Josie's room and when we go in, Bernie is drinking her brandy and Josie has make-up on. Bernie said they had their last party. After Bernie leaves we all sit solemn and reflect. As we talked I looked at Josie and saw her last breath. The nurse had told me when it happened to tell her. I held her and said "I'll always love you." Linda said her good-bye and I called Terry and Bernie and told them it was over. I went to the nurse's station and told them. They looked at the clock and it was two minutes after midnight. They said they had to call it the eighth because that's when I told them. It was really the seventh. I used the hall phone and called Annette and told her to tell her Sonny. After so many years you know he had to love her like a sister, even if they fought. Before I left Tucson I had put together my black outfit and told Annette to bring it to me.

Back to the room and Rudy was still holding Josie. Benny and Linda left. I held Rudy and told him let go, they have a lot to do. We drove home in the rain and when we got to Josie's, Robert got there and we had a few drinks and talked and then I went to bed.

The next day we had to go to the cemetery and pay it off, Terry, Bernie, my brother Fud and I. Fud had come down to take us wherever we had to go. They leave me at Josie's and Terry and Bernie go to the mortuary where they prepared Josie. Josie had wanted my dress that she had borrowed for her son's wedding. She said that was the happiest day of her life. They took it. Now Bernie and Terry fix Josie in a wig and put on her makeup. I was sleeping. Sonny and my son

Rudy get there, followed by Annette and her husband David. She brought my outfit.

When the wake began, all Lincoln Heights was there. Family, friends and co-workers. From the back of the room, oldies but goodies played. It was the first time one of the girls had died and we all felt it. When I looked at Josie, she looked beautiful and in her hands was a copy of "A Tree Grows in Brooklyn."

It was a long, empty night. The next morning when the limo came to pick up everyone, I stayed to go with Sonny and my son. When we got to Sacred Heart Church, it was packed. Sonny was a pallbearer and Bernie and Terry and I walked in with the coffin. We sat and listened as my brother Fud once more said the eulogy and told everyone that Josie would want everyone to party. The couple sang "Seek Ye First" and "Amazing Grace" for her. Off to the cemetery and the service there. The priest was very nice and he had met her so he talked to her. He asked me who gets the cross and I pointed to her beloved son, Rudy.

After the service everyone comes to console me and I take a tranquilizer. I hugged and said good-byes. Everyone is gong to Josie's house where the food has been prepared. I went to her coffin and touched it and said, "Bye Jo." I got in the car with Annette and David and never looked back. I sat in the back with my granddaughter, now called Rae Rae, and slept. We drove home and never went back to that house again. My two daughters, Christy and Suzette, gave birth the next month and when Suzette was in trouble with the birth, I felt Josie and knew she would be all right.

I went into a depression and had many afternoons sitting in my den crying for no reason. My weight went up and I could find no comfort in life. I did not realize what was happening so I fought against going for help. My daughters pushed me to the doctors and I found my doctor, Dr. Callingham, who was smarter than me. She spotted the depression and even though I said I was fine, she knew better. Off I got to a psychiatrist and I remember entering his office thinking, "I'm not telling him anything. Thinks he's going to get me to talk." I think I was there for five minutes and I was telling him everything. I saw him every week and was given an anti-depressant to put back the hormone that is damaged with a depression. I will be on it the rest of my life.

The reason I'm telling you all this is so you will realize that the strongest of women can fall. Women have all the weight on their shoulders and they carry it. They must run the family, handle all crises, and never reflect the fear. This is a bunch of bull and I want women to admit when "they have had it" without being made to feel ashamed. It is like the doctor said, "When the garbage can is full, it will overflow." This is what happened to me.

And so, my Josie, I hope I have told our story and maybe someone out in the world of hopelessness will see there is a life over the hill.

WE IS NOW I

We is now I, and memories that remain of a life so filled with

friends, family, and love, now flow away like the wind.

Have they gone to sleep?

Or are they waiting to be rekindled after death?

New memories must be my own,

and none can quite live up to my memories of days gone by.

Friends and family leave, and a void is left

that is like an open wound which will not heal.

There is an emptiness that comes with age,

and a feeling of sadness you camouflage.

Places you enjoyed are now places of memories that hurt.

And in my solitude, you, my friend, come to me.

—-Nellie Altamirano Bustillos

About the Author

Nellie has lived a life filled with family secrets, family filled with history. She graduated from Roosevelt high school in Los Angeles California in 1959. She attended Mount San Antonio Jr College in 1970-72. She later returned to school in Tucson Arizona attending Pima Community College where she majored in history. She next attended the University of Arizona where she majored in history and political science. She has received awards from the University of Arizona alumni association, Phi Theta Kappa Tucson bilingual association. She has done much research in the history of her family, Sepulveda of Los Angeles, Zepeda of Tucson and has lived history in her adventure of life.